MASTER OF

EDITED BY
Graham Brooks
Chris Irwin

IRON MAKING IN CUMBRIA

PROCEEDINGS OF A JOINT CONFERENCE OF THE CUMBRIA INDUSTRIAL HISTORY SOCIETY AND THE HISTORICAL METALLURGY SOCIETY

THE CUMBRIA INDUSTRIAL SOCIETY 2007

CONTENTS

IRON ORE IN CUMBRIA   5
BY BRIAN YOUNG

ARCHAEOLOGICAL INVESTIGATION AT   27
CUNSEY FORGE: AN INTERIM REPORT
BY IAN MILLER

THE BLOOMSMITHIES OF SOUTH   49
WESTMORLAND AND NORTH LANCASHIRE
BY RICHARD NEWMAN

WILSON HOUSE LINDALE: JOHN   65
WILKINSON'S PEAT FUELLED BLAST
FURNACE
BY DAVID CRANSTONE

HODBARROW MINE—AN INDUSTRY   93
WITHIN AN INDUSTRY.
BY ERIC HOLLAND

MILLOM—THE END GAME   107
BY DAVID ROBSON DAVIS

BACKBARROW FURNACE AND ITS   117
HISTORY 1868 - 1967
BY MIKE DAVIES-SHIEL.

First published 2007 by

The Cumbria Industrial History Society
C/o Mr. Graham Brooks
Coomara
Carleton
Carlisle
CA4 0BU

Tel: 01228 537379
Fax: 01228 596986

EMAIL gbrooksvet@tiscali.co.uk

Web site www.cumbria-industries.org.uk

©The Cumbria Industrial History Society and the authors 2007. All rights of reproduction reserved.

ISBN 978-0-9533799-6-5

THE CUMBRIAN INDUSTRIAL HISTORY SOCIETY

CIHS was formed in 1985 by members of the Cumberland and Westmorland Antiquarian and Archaeological Society with a particular interest in industrial history. The regular programme includes winter evening meetings, guided field trips in summer, often to sites closed to the public, two one day conferences and a regular Bulletin. In addition, the Society is actively involved in the recording and conservation of important IA sites.
Further details may be obtained from the membership secretary;

Roger Baker
4 Barnes Cottage
Back Lane
Preesall
Poulton FY6 0HT

IRON ORE IN CUMBRIA

By Brian Young
British Geological Survey
(Present address: Department of Earth Science, University of Durham, Science Laboratories, South Road, Durham DH1 3LE (e-mail: brian.young@hotmail.co uk))

INTRODUCTION

Over the centuries Cumbria has been a prolific source of a variety of metal ores and related minerals (Cooper and Stanley, 1990; Dunham, 1990; Young, 1987). The most valuable of these has been iron ore. Huge deposits of high grade iron ore, and abundant local coal, fed the iron and steel making plants which were the basis of the county's former heavy industries which reached their peak during the 19th century. Although still major elements in the county's economy during the opening years of the 20th century, an inexorable and inevitable decline in the industry's fortunes had by then already set in, a decline that was to witness the virtual extinction of these traditional industries in the second half of the 20th century. Yet the industry was reluctant to die completely. Despite the abandonment of large-scale iron ore mining in the 1970s, Cumbria remained Britain's sole commercial source of iron ore, though its working was, by then, the merest shadow of its distinguished past. A tiny output of haematite ore was maintained from a shallow, and hitherto largely unworked, portion of the orebody at Florence Mine, Egremont. Much of this meagre output was employed in specialised steel making as well as in the pigment trade. At the time of writing (November 2006), it seems certain that pumping will soon be discontinued at Florence, with the inevitable result that the mine will rapidly flood and become permanently inaccessible. Thus will end centuries of iron ore working in Cumbria.

In order to fully understand the origins of iron making in Cumbria, and its development over the centuries, it is essential to have an appreciation of the distribution of iron ores within the county, and an understanding of the nature of those occurrences and of the ore types found there.

Presented here is a brief review of the distribution and geological setting of the iron ores, together with comments on their most distinctive characteristics. It is hoped that this will assist in understanding the pattern of known archaeological evidence for the iron industry and that it might serve to direct research to areas hitherto unexplored for evidence of iron making. Descriptions of the characteristics of individual ore types may aid interpretation of materials encountered during archaeological investigations of iron working sites.

GEOLOGICAL BACKGROUND

Cumbria's rocks record evidence of complex geological events over at least 500 million years of Earth history. Space does not permit a review of this great geological diversity, though Figure 1 presents a highly simplified picture of the geology. A useful summary of the county's geology is available in the Geochemical Atlas for the Lake District (British Geological Survey, 1992). More detailed descriptions of individual areas are published in the relevant BGS Sheet Memoirs.

THE IRON ORES

Three main types of iron ore have been worked in Cumbria, each of which is distinctive and confined to a particular geological environment. In addition, local occurrences of several iron-rich minerals, in other geological settings, deserve comment. Although these are not known to have been exploited as ores, their presence may be worthy of consideration when attempting to identify small local supplies of ore, particular with regard to early smelting sites remote from other known sources of ore.

Haematite ores:

Best known of the Cumbrian iron ores are the haematite ores, which were the basis of the iron and steel industries of the 19th and 20th centuries. These are concentrated within two major ore-fields: the West Cumbrian Orefield, between Lamplugh and Egremont, and the South Cumbrian Orefield in the Millom and Furness area. At least 250 million tonnes of haematite ore have been raised from these two orefields since the middle of the 19th century (Rose and Dunham, 1977). Metallic iron contents of up to a little over 60% were obtained from the best west Cumbrian ores: slightly lower iron contents of up to 57% were recorded from south Cumbria. In addition, a number of very scattered deposits of haematite ores occur within the Lake District fells. The distribution of this haematite mineralisation within Cumbria is shown of Figure 2. Although there are some significant differences between the deposits in each of these areas, the geological and mineralogical characteristics clearly indicate that they are expressions of one major province of haematite mineralisation.

These deposits have attracted geological attention from an

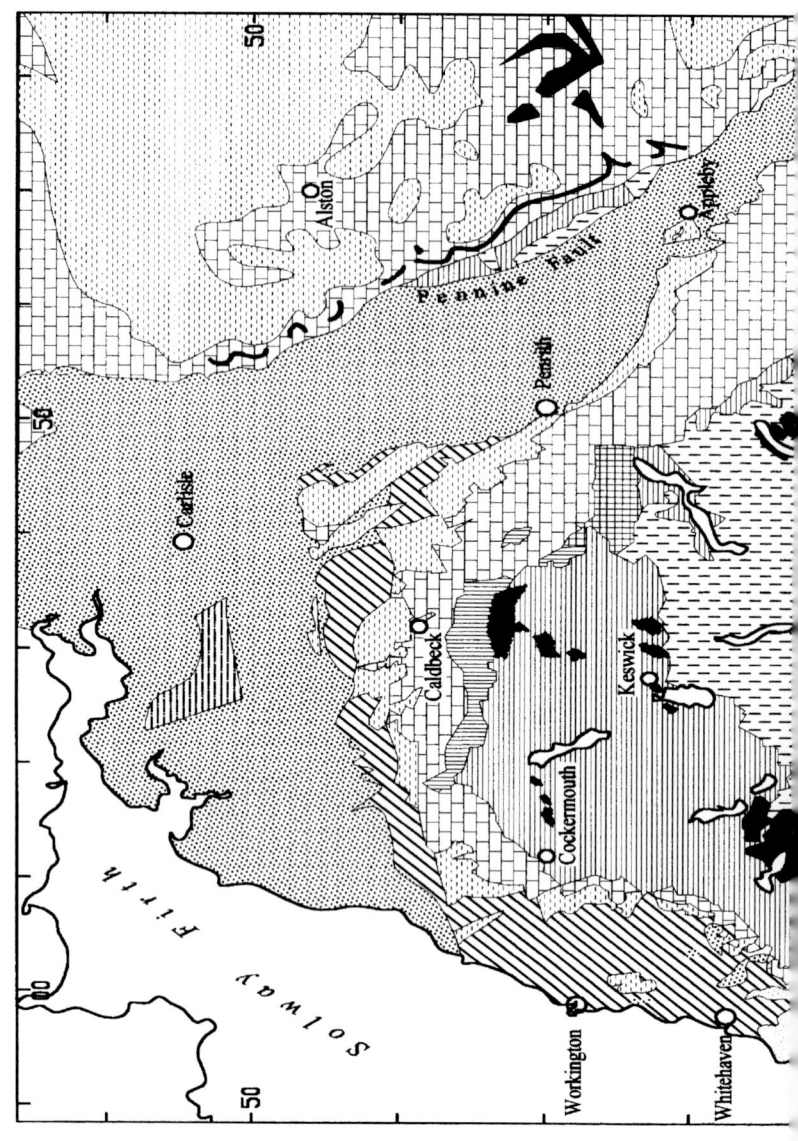

Figure 1. Simplified geological map of Cumbria

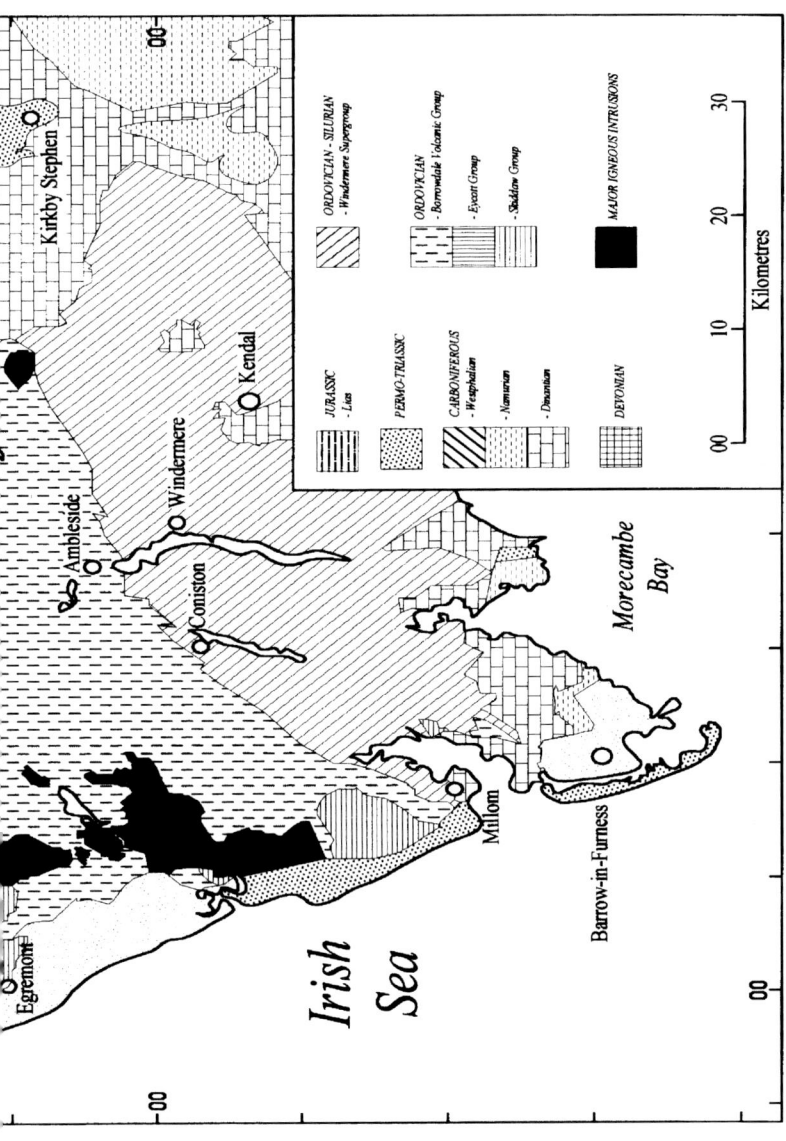

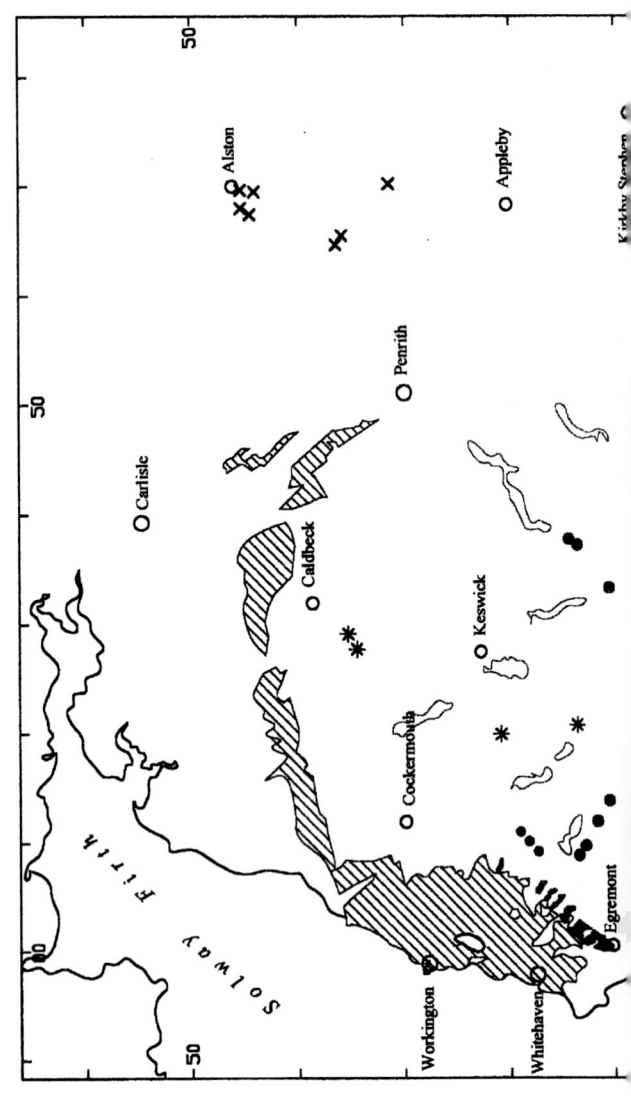

Figure 2. Iron ore occurrences in Cumbria

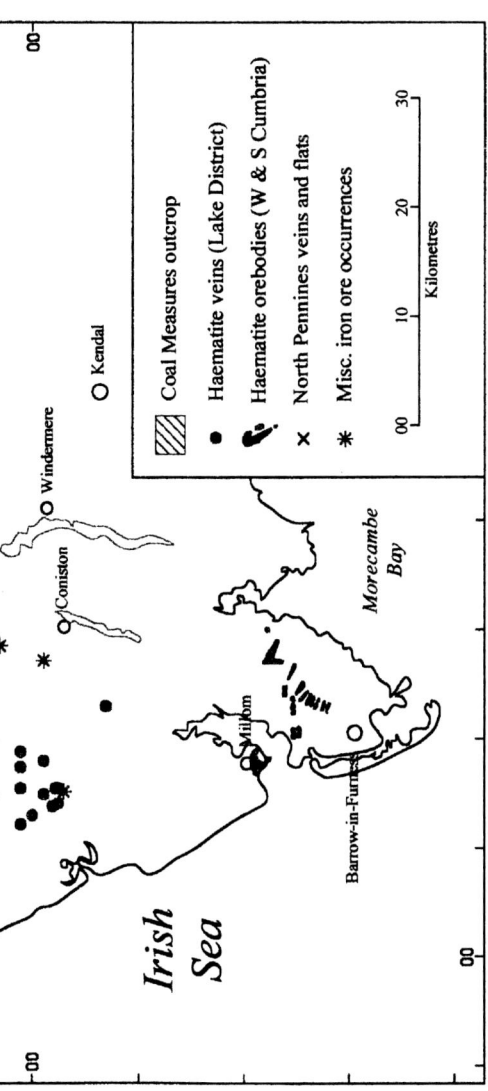

early date. Descriptions of the orefields, including details of individual mines, include those of Kendall (1893), Smith (1924) and Dunham and Rose (1941). More recent accounts, including modern views on the origins of the deposits, include works by Rose and Dunham (1977), Dunham (1985), and Shepherd and Goldring (1993). References to the very substantial volume of technical literature are to be found in these texts.

The haematite deposits of the west and south Cumbrian orefields mainly occur as large, irregular or flat-lying replacements of Lower Carboniferous (Dinantian) limestones, usually closely associated with, or adjacent to, faults. The local presence of fossils and other features within the parent limestone, completely or partly replaced by haematite, clearly demonstrates the replacement origin for these ores.

The west Cumbrian orefield may be considered in two parts. North of Egremont the Carboniferous limestones, which contain the main orebodies, are exposed at the surface where they form a narrow rim to the coalfield. Although the numerous mines of this area followed the orebodies to considerable depths below surface, there can be no doubt that surface exposures of haematite would have been conspicuous and readily discovered by the earliest iron makers. South of Egremont, and extending almost to Calder Bridge, orebodies within the Carboniferous limestones which lie concealed beneath the cover of Permo-Triassic rocks were discovered during mine development and exploration in the late 19th and early 20th centuries. The earliest iron workers could not have discovered these deposits. Florence Mine, at Egremont, the area's last surviving mine, worked a haematite body concealed beneath Permo-Triassic rocks.

Very similar orebodies characterise much of the south Cumbrian orefield, though the Furness area contains numerous haematite bodies known as 'sops'. In these deposits, which are unique to Furness, haematite fills large, roughly conical dissolution hollows in the limestone. The centre of each 'sop' is typically filled with sand. As in west Cumbria, exposures of haematite ore, contrasting strikingly with pale limestone, would have attracted the attention of the earliest iron workers. Small pockets of haematite could, until recently, still be seen within the limestones exposed at Hodbarrow Point.

The Lower Palaeozoic rocks of the Lake District fells locally contain fissure veins filled with haematite. The greatest concentrations of these are to be found in Eskdale and Ennerdale, where significant mines worked until the early years of the 20th century. Other clusters of related haematite mineralisation occur in the Esk Pike area, notably around the appropriately named Ore Gap and Red Tarn; parts of the Buttermere Fells; Tongue Gill, near Grasmere; and Deepdale, Patterdale. Conspicuous red haematite-staining of fractured rock along faults and fissures within the Lower Palaeozoic rocks is comparatively widespread throughout the Lake District, giving rise to common local names such as Red Pike, Red Tarn etc. Except in a few localities, this haematisation is usually no more than an intense reddening of the fractured rocks, though small concentrations of solid haematite may occur locally.

Common to all of these deposits is their mineralogical composition. Haematite, in a variety of forms, is everywhere the dominant mineral. Compact, massive haematite with a characteristic bluish grey or bluish purple colour is extremely common, particularly in the west and south Cumbrian fields. A rather softer, dull red, massive or brecciated, locally rather earthy, form of the mineral also occurs, particularly in parts of the south Cumbrian field. The term 'smit' is sometimes applied to the very softest forms of this ore. Perhaps the best known, and most distinctive, variety of Cumbrian haematite is the fibrous reniform variety known as 'kidney ore'. This is common in many of the west and south Cumbrian deposits, and is also abundant in the related vein deposits within the Lake District fells. Indeed, it is the dominant variety of the mineral in the Ennerdale and Eskdale mines and those in Deepdale, near Patterdale. Whereas much of this variety from west and south Cumbria consists of comparatively large 'kidneys', up to several centimetres across, smaller 'kidneys', commonly less than 1 centimetre across, are very common in ore from many of the Lake District veins. 'Kidney ore' breaks readily into distinctive elongate conical fragments, known to Cumbrian miners as 'pencil ore'. Even in very small fragments, this highly distinctive form can often be a good clue to the origins of the sample. The Cumbrian deposits locally contain small concentrations of well-crystallised haematite, known as specularite, usually as distinctive small (up to 2 millimetres) tabular black crystals with a very high lustre. The highly characteristic, and extremely persistent, bright red colour of crushed haematite, and its tendency to colour everything with which it has been in contact, is another excellent clue to identifying these ore types.

A notable feature of all of the Cumbrian haematite deposits is the scarcity of gangue minerals. This is especially so in the veins of the Lake District. In these, very small amounts of quartz, and, locally, extremely small quantities of manganese oxide minerals, baryte and calcite, comprise the only visible gangue minerals. Gangue minerals in the replacement deposits in the limestones include dolomite, calcite, quartz, pyrite and, in west Cumbria, baryte, fluorite and, very locally, siderite. Although these minerals may appear conspicuous on mine spoil heaps, they almost invariably comprise an extremely small proportion of the orebodies. Small, but economically recoverable concentrations of managese oxide minerals were present within the orebody at Bigrigg Mine, Egremont, and copper sulphide minerals were recovered from a unique deposit associated with the haematite orebody at Anty Cross Mine, Dalton-in-Furness.

Clay ironstones:

Nodules, or discontinuous bands, of impure siderite, or 'clay iron stone' are common in the Coal Measures (Westphalian) of the Cumbrian Coalfield, the outcrop of which is shown in Figure 2 (Eastwood, 1930; Eastwood et al, 1931; Young and Armstrong, 1989; Boland and Young, 1992). Most commonly these occur as scattered nodules in beds of mudstone or clay, and usually range in size from pellets a few millimetres across to ovoid or ball-shaped masses up to 30 centimetres across. More uncommonly, such ironstones are found in sandstones, for example in the Countess Pit Sandstone exposed in the cliffs between Whitehaven and Parton, where they occur as conglomeratic masses (Eastwood et al, 1931). Barnes et al (1986) described sphaerosiderite-rich nodules in the mudstones below the Black Metal Coal in Lostrigg Beck, Little Clifton.

Eastwood et al (1931) also note the occurrence of clay ironstone nodules within mudstones now included within the Hensingham Group (Namurian) in the Bigrigg, Cleator Moor, Hensingham, and Workington areas.

Cumbrian clay ironstones typically contain up to around 25% metallic iron, and are thus substantially lower in grade than the haematite ores. As these are carbonate ores they require calcining prior to smelting. In view of these properties, and their occurrence, normally scattered through beds of mudstone, they are much less attractive as commercial ores and thus appear to have been worked only locally and on a small scale. Cantrill (1920) mentions the working of clay ironstone nodules, locally known as 'catscopes', from the mudstones above the Metal Band Seam at Clifton Colliery, Great Clifton, and notes that, from about 1873, similar ores were raised from collieries at Flimby, Melgramfitz and Ellenborough. Total annual production of such ores in the 19th century appears to have reached a little over 1000 tons, though no production is recorded after 1909.

Although never approaching the commercial importance of haematite ores, clay ironstones are very likely to have attracted the interest of early iron makers. Although not generally well-exposed, the Coal Measures rocks of Cumbria do crop out in a number of stream sections and coastal cliffs between Workington and Whitehaven, and Hensingham Group rocks are exposed around Hensingham. Clay ironstone nodules also occur locally within the Carboniferous shales of the Northern Pennines. These nodules are likely to have been easily seen in exposures and, since they are generally much more resistant to weathering than the enclosing mudstones, are likely to have been conspicuous in soils derived from the weathering of such outcrops.

Clay ironstones normally consist of segregations of impure, fine grained siderite with a high clay content. Most nodules are roughly spherical or flattened ovoids which may be up to around 30 centimetres across, though most are smaller. When weathered, the nodules typically exhibit a rusty brown outer coating which serves to distinguish them from the surrounding mudstone. When freshly broken they are usually medium to dark grey in colour with a dull stony appearance. When the spherulitic variety of siderite, known as sphaerosiderite, is present, the ironstone assumes a rather granular appearance. Deeply weathered nodules are brown throughout, the colour sometimes being developed in concentric bands parallel to the outer surfaces of the nodule. Their weight is noticeable. Some ironstone nodules display septarian structure, in which a complex pattern of more or less radial internal cracks are lined or filled with white or cream calcite or ankerite, in many instances accompanied by soft white earthy kaolinite.

Vein iron ores of the Northern Pennines:

The numerous veins and associated replacement, or 'flat', deposits of the Northern Pennines, in eastern Cumbria, are perhaps best known as sources of lead ores. However, iron mineralisation is common in almost all of these deposits and is locally present in workable quantities (Cantrill et al 1919; Dunham, 1941; 1990). The main locations for such ores are indicated in Figure 2.

Within the fissure veins, the iron carbonate minerals siderite and ankerite are commonly important components of the gangue assemblage accompanying lead and zinc ores. Where the veins cut limestone, metasomatic alteration of the wallrock to an ankerite- or siderite-rich rock is very common. This alteration may extend laterally through the limestone for many metres on one or both sides of the parent vein, forming the extensive replacement bodies known to the Northern Pennine miners as 'flats'. These flats typically contain rich concentrations of sulphide ores, mainly galena and/or sphalerite, together with pockets of gangue minerals such as fluorite or baryte. Many deposits of this sort in the Cumbrian

Pennines have been important producers of lead and zinc ores.

The mineral deposits of the Cumbrian Pennines are comparatively well-exposed and are known to have attracted early historical attention as sources of lead, and associated silver. The abundance within many of them of conspicuous concentrations of iron minerals almost certainly attracted interest from early iron workers. Documentary records exist for 12th century iron mining from exactly similar deposits in the Rookhope area of Weardale.

Siderite and ankerite readily weather to iron oxide and hydroxide minerals, to which the collective term 'limonite' is commonly applied. In older literature the term 'brown haematite' is commonly used to describe these limonitic ores, though use of this term should be strongly discouraged as haematite is rarely, if ever, present. The resultant bodies of iron oxides are usually significantly richer in iron than the original carbonate minerals. Metallic iron contents of up to 48% are quoted for these ores. Although essentially unweathered iron carbonate ores have been successfully worked as iron ores in parts of the Northern Pennines, both from veins and flats, the greatest tonnages of iron ore from these deposits has been derived from completely, or almost completely oxidised ores. Several deposits of this sort have been worked in eastern Cumbria, for example at the Ardale Head and nearby mines on the Pennine escarpment, and at the Park and Nest mines near Alston. Substantial quantities of oxidised iron ores occur within the the Dun Fell Veins, and associated flat deposits, in the huge opencut known as Dun Fell Hush, near the summit of Great Dun Fell. The oxidised deposit at Horse Edge, SW of Alston, yielded umber, a soft form of 'limonite', for use as a pigment. Figures for iron ore output from this part of Cumbria are incomplete, though Cantrill et al (1919) record the annual output of iron ore from Alston Moor peaking at over 17 000 tons in 1858. Subsequent years saw production at much lower levels, on occasions amounting to only a few hundred tons per year: no production figures are given for the years after 1875.

In veins, siderite and ankerite commonly form moderately to coarsely crystalline masses, with well-formed curved saddle-shaped rhombic crystals lining cavities. Siderite/ankerite rock from flat deposits, when unweathered, can resemble unaltered limestone, though closer examination reveals a rather coarser crystalline texture than is normal in most of the area's limestones. Cavities lined with characteristic curved rhombs may be common, and spots or bands of sulphides such as galena or sphalerite, or pockets of fluorite or baryte, may be present. Fresh siderite and ankerite are white or pale cream in colour, though some oxidation is almost invariably present giving a variety of brownish tints to the mineral. It is impossible to discriminate between siderite and ankerite in the field, though the more intense oxidation of siderite is a useful, though by no means always reliable, first indication of composition.

Limonitic iron ores from the Cumbrian Pennines are typically massive, compact or earthy, dark brown in colour and often form rather cavernous or porous masses. Locally, for example at Ardale Head, thin bands (up to a few millimetres thick) of crystalline goethite, in places with glossy, mammillated surfaces, can be seen. Many samples of such ores exhibit clear pseudomorphs after small, curved, saddle-shaped rhombic crystals of the primary ankerite or siderite, from which the oxidised ore was derived. Dunham (1990) describes masses of limonitic ore with unaltered cores of limestone at the Nest Mines, Alston.

Miscellaneous occurrences of iron minerals:

A variety of other iron-bearing minerals, with at least some theoretical potential as iron ores, occur at various places within Cumbria. Although there is no evidence to suggest any working of these as iron ores, the occurrences may warrant consideration in attempting to identify small sources of iron ore, particularly at early smelting sites. The main localities for these minerals are shown in Figure 2.

A small number of the copper-bearing veins of the Coniston area locally contain appreciable quantities of magnetite. This mineral is an important iron ore in many parts of the world, though no substantial deposits of it have ever been successfully exploited in Britain. Best known of these Lake District magnetite-rich deposits is the Bonsor Vein of the Coniston Copper Mines (Dagger, 1977; Stanley and Vaughan, 1982). However, the mineral seems to occur only at deep levels within the vein and may not have been present in the surface outcrops. Magnetite is, however, present in substantial concentrations in the Long Crag Vein, exposed high on the south side of the Greenburn Valley (Stanley and Vaughan, 1982). Magnetite, locally accompanied by specular haematite, has recently been described as a major constituent of veins in Wasdale (Millward et al, 1999) and in Eskdale (Young, 1985). Small trial workings, thought to have been made in search of copper ore, occur at the two former localities. It is conceivable that early iron makers may have recognised and used magnetite from one or more of these sites.

Veins of coarse-grained specular haematite, which from their form and paragenesis appear unrelated to the main Cumbrian haematite mineralisation discussed above, occur at Devoke

Water (Young, 1985) and Honister (Moon and Wildridge, 1969: Millward et al, 1999). There are no signs of any workings at the former locality and, although a short trial level of unknown date has been driven on the vein at the latter locality, nothing is known of any ore production.

Siderite is a comparatively abundant constituent in the lower levels of the Force Crag lead-zinc vein vein in Coledale and iron oxide minerals occur in the uppermost workings of this vein (Young, 1987). Goethite is common at several sites on the Caldbeck Fells, including the Roughton Gill South Vein at the foot of the appropriately named Iron Crags and at the Harestones Umber Mine, where earthy iron oxide was formerly worked as a pigment (Cooper and Stanley, 1990). Limonite-rich gossans may formerly have marked the outcrop of several of the copper-bearing veins of the Lake District. A remaining example may today be seen on the Thriddle Vein outcrop at Coniston (Millward et al, 2000). All may conceivably have attracted the attention of the early iron makers, though amounts of any useable ore are likely to have been extremely small, and probably difficult to smelt.

Bog ores:

Discussion of early iron making amongst industrial archaeologists commonly involves speculation over the working of 'bog ores', especially where smelting sites are remote from known occurrences of iron ores.

Bog ores are accumulations of iron oxide or hydroxide minerals, formed by the concentration of iron in swamp or soil pore-waters through the stabilizing effect of organic materials (Young, 1993). There appear to be no records of bog ore occurrences in Cumbria. There is little geological evidence for their presence on any significant scale, and it seems highly unlikely that the county contains, or ever contained, accumulations of such materials sufficient to sustain even the tiniest smelting operation.

Closely related are concentrations of iron oxide and hydroxide minerals in 'iron pans' in superficial deposits. In Cumbria such iron pans appear to be very localised and generally extremely limited in extent, with a very high concentration of included sand, gravel and cobbles, and almost certainly with a low iron content. It is unlikely that these ever yielded usable ore.

Acknowledgements

Peter Young is thanked for preparing the maps. This paper is published with the approval of the Executive Director, British Geological Survey (N.E.R.C.)

REFERENCES

BARNES, R.P., YOUNG, B., FROST, D.V. and LAND, D.H. 1986. The geology of Workington and Maryport. *British Geological Survey Technical Report* No.WA/88/3.

BOLAND, M.P. and YOUNG, B. 1992. Geology and land-use planning: Great Broughton-Lamplugh area, Cumbria. *British Geological Survey Technical Report No. WA/92/55*

BRITISH GEOLOGICAL SURVEY. 1992. Regional geochemistry of the Lake District and adjacent areas. *Keyworth, British Geological Survey.*

CANTRILL, T.C. *in* STRAHAN, A., GIBSON, W., SHERLOCK, R.L. and DEWEY, H. 1920. Pre-Carboniferous and Carboniferous bedded iron-ores of England and Wales. *Special Reports of the Mineral Resources of Great Britain, Memoir of the Geological Survey of Great Britain.*

CANTRILL, T.C., SHERLOCK, R.L. and DEWEY, H. 1919. Iron ores. Sundry unbedded ores of Durham, East Cumberland, North Wales, Derbyshire, the Isle of Man, Bristol District and Somerset, Devon and Cornwall. *Special Reports of the Mineral Resources of Great Britain, Memoir of the Geological Survey of Great Britain.*

COOPER, M.P. and STANLEY, C.J. 1990. *Minerals of the English Lake District – Caldbeck Fells.* London, British Museum (Natural History).

DAGGER, G.W. 1977. Controls of copper mineralization at Consiton, English Lake District. *Geological Magazine,* Vol. 114, pp 195-202.

DUNHAM, K.C. 1941. Iron ore deposits of the Northern Pennines. *Wartime Pamphlet of the Geological Survey of Great Britain* No. 14.

DUNHAM, K.C. 1985. Genesis of the Cumbrian hematite deposits. *Proceedings of the Yorkshire Geological Society,* Vol. 45, p 130.

DUNHAM, K.C. 1990. Geology of the Northern Pennine Orefield Vol. 1 Tyne to Stainmore. *Economic Memoir of the British Geological Survey.*

DUNHAM, K.C. and ROSE, W.C.C. 1941. Geology of the iron ore field of south Cumberland and Furness. *Wartime Pamphlet of the Geological Survey of Great Britain* No. 16.

EASTWOOD, T. 1930. The geology of the Maryport district. *Memoir of the Geologoical Survey of Great Britain.*

EASTWOOD, T., DIXON, E.E.L., HOLLINGWORTH, S.E. and SMITH, B. 1931. The geology of the Whitehaven and Workington district. *Memoir of the Geologoical Survey of Great Britain.*

KENDALL, J.D. 1893. *The Iron Ores of Great Britain and Ireland.* London, Crosby Lockwood.

MILLWARD, D., BEDDOE-STEPHENS, B. and YOUNG, B. 1999. Pre-Acadian copper mineralisation in the English Lake District. *Geological Magazine.* Vol. 136, pp 159-176.

MILLWARD, D., JOHNSON, E.W., BEDDOE-STEPHENS, B., YOUNG, B., KNELLER, B.C., LEE, M.K., ALLEN, P.M., BRANNEY, M.J., COOPER, D.C., HIRONS, S., KOKELAAR, B.P., MARKS, R.J., McCONNELL, B.J., MERRITT, J.W., MOLYNEUEX, S.G., PETTERSON, M.G., ROBERTS, B., RUNDLE, C.C., RUSHTON, A.W.A., SCOTT, R.W., SOPER, N.J. and STONE, P. 2000. Geology of the Ambleside district. *Memoir of the British Geological Survey.*

MOON, J.R. and WILDRIDGE, J.D.J. 1969. The geology and non-ferrous mines of the Buttermere and Loweswater Valleys. *Memoirs of the Northern Cavern and Mine Research Society* 1968, pp 38-51.

ROSE, W.C.C. and DUNHAM, K.C. 1977. Geology and hematite deposits of South Cumbria. *Economic Memoir of the Geological Survey of Great Britain.*

SHEPHERD, T.J. and GOLDRING, D.C. 1993. Cumbrian hematite deposits, North-west England. pp 419-445 In. PATTRICK, R.A.D. and POLYA, D.A. (editors) *Mineralization in the British Isles.* London, Chapman & Hall.

SMITH, B. 1924. Iron ores. Haematites of West Cumberland, Lancashire and the Lake District. *Special Reports of the Mineral Resources of Great Britain, Memoir of the Geological Survey of Great Britain.*

STANLEY, C.J. and VAUGHAN, D.J. 1982. Mineralization in the Bonser Vein, Coniston, English Lake District: mineral assemblages, paragenesis and formation conditions. *Mineralogical*

Magazine, Vol. 46, pp 343-350.

YOUNG, B. 1985. Mineralisation associated with the Eskdale Intrusion, Cumbria. *Lake District Regional Geological Survey Report. Report of Programme Directorate A, British Geological Survey,* No. PDA2 85/3.

YOUNG, B. 1987. *Glossary of the minerals of the Lake District and adjoining areas.* Newcastle upon Tyne, British Geological Survey.

YOUNG, B. and ARMSTRONG, M. 1989. The applied geological mapping of the Dearham and Gilcrux area, Cumbria. *British Geological Survey Technical Report* No. WA/89/70.

YOUNG, T. 1993. Sedimentary iron ores. pp 446-489. In PATTRICK, R.A.D. and POLYA, D.A. (editors) *Mineralization in the British Isles.* London, Chapman & Hall.

ARCHAEOLOGICAL INVESTIGATIONS AT CUNSEY FORGE: AN INTERIM REPORT

By Ian Miller
Oxford Archaeology North
Lancaster

Introduction

During January 2003, Oxford Archaeology North undertook an archaeological investigation of part of Cunsey forge, Cumbria, on behalf of the Lake District National Park Authority (LDNPA). The work was required to examine and record the features and deposits that had been exposed during the recent demolition of a stone building which occupied the west part of the former forge complex.

Cunsey bloomforge (ie a water-powered, direct smelting and refining site with several hearths) was established in 1618, although there is some evidence for the existence of a bloomsmithy (i.e. a water-powered, direct smelting site with a single hearth) in the area since the mid-16th century. The bloomforge was remodelled as a refining forge in 1715, which remained in production until c1762. Much of the forge was demolished in c1800, although a linear range of stone buildings survived largely intact until the 1980s.

The archaeological investigation comprised the clearance of rubble from part of the site, combined with a programme of localised excavation, rectified photography, and limited geophysical survey. An appraisal of the available documentary sources was also undertaken to enhance the results of the fieldwork.

This paper presents an interim report of the investigation, in advance of further detailed analysis.

SITE LOCATION

Cunsey forge (centred on NGR SD 37766 49361) is located some 5km SE of Hawkshead, within the Furness district of Cumbria (formerly Lancashire North of the Sands). The forge lies at a height of c60m OD, and is situated on the south side of Cunsey Beck, which flows into lake Windermere a little over 1km to the west (Fig 1).

The site is encompassed by tracts of mixed woodland and copses; the woodlands to the west and south-west, known as Great Ore Gate and Little Ore Gate respectively, comprise coniferous plantation, although both also contain dense groups of hardwood species, some of which have been coppiced.

DOCUMENTARY EVIDENCE

Origins

The earliest reference to ironworking at Cunsey is embodied in a document of 1549, cited by Fell (1908, 181-3), which refers to 'Constey Smythy'. However, the exact location of this bloomsmithy is not specified.

The origins of Cunsey bloomforge may be traced to March 1618, when William Wright, the leading figure of the 17th century Cumbrian iron industry, acquired a lease of land at Cunsey on which to build an ironworks (Phillips 1977, 37). A further lease (LRO DDSa 2/5), pursuant to that of March 1618, was issued on 2 September 1621 by Katherin Sands of

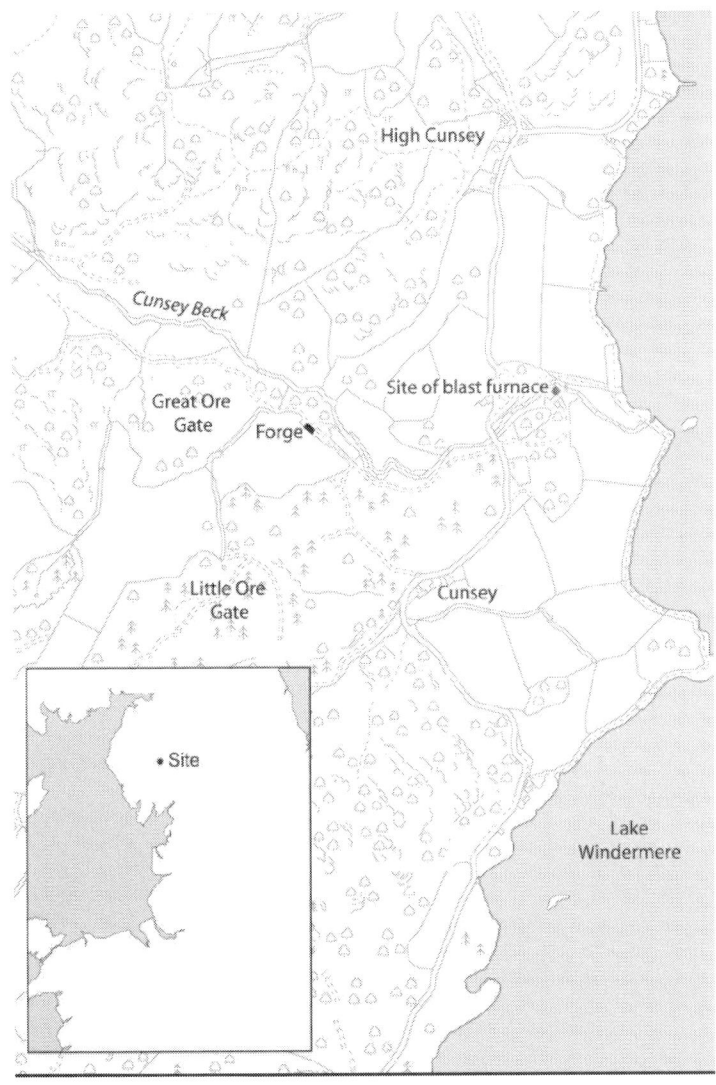

Fig. 1 Location map.

Grathwait to William Wright of Consay, *'hammerman'*. The lease was for 18 years at £10 rent, and incorporated 'two acres of ground by Consay Beck, with a forge, other buildings, a dam already made in the beck, banks on both sides of the dam, liberty to pound and stay the water, way to Consay mill and Windermeer [sic] water, liberty to get "sodds and stones" and "grubbe up" woods and trees near the dam, with bloomsmithy and colehouse'. The details of this lease suggest that, by 1621, the site comprised not only a forge, but also a bloomsmithy, apparently as a separate component.

The finery and chafery

On 2 May 1639, an agreement between Gawen Brathwait and William Wright documents the proposed division of the forge (LRO DDSa 2/11). Under the terms, Gawen Brathwait was to have the *'upper finerie'* and William Wright to have the *'chafferie'* and *'lower finerie'*, indicating the forge to have been equipped at an early stage with both finery and chafery hearths. Evidence for other structures on the site during this period is provided by an indenture, issued on 20 June 1647 between William Wright and his son, Alexander Wright, and Rowland ?Lawson (CRO(B) BD/HJ/89/8). This refers to 'the fforge [sic] or Iron Works at Consey commonly called Consey fforge together with one dwelling house one coal house one stable one house for iron and all other houses, buildings, floodgates...'.

Ironmasters after William Wright

Upon the expiry of his lease in 1659, William Wright relinquished the Cunsey works (PRO PL 6/22). Information regarding subsequent occupiers, however, is provided by entries in the Hawkshead parish register (1568-1704). An early entry is for Charles Russell 'of Consey', whose name first appears in 1665 (Cowper 1897, 275). The Russells were a notable family of ironworkers, who had emigrated from Normandy to Sussex *c* 1520, and have been traced to ironworks in Yorkshire before arriving in Cumbria in *c* 1630 (Awty and Phillips 1980, 33).

Fell claims that Charles Russell left Cunsey for Coniston forge in 1675 (1908, 192), although 'Charles Russell de Consay forge' appears several times in the Hawkshead parish register until 1690 (Cowper 1897). Moreover, a partnership between Myles Sandys, Richard Washington of Kirkby Kendall, and Charles Russell of Cunsey, referring to the business of making and selling iron at Cunsey forge, was issued on 19 October 1681 (LRO DDSa 38/1). Each partner agreed to contribute £100 to joint stock at the forge, which doubtless represented a fairly substantial investment.

Subsequent entries in the Hawkshead parish register include Emanuell Ellattson 'de Consey forge', who appears in 1696, whilst in 1698 and 1703, Clement Holme of 'Consey forge' is entered. John Massocks, who had been employed at Force forge in 1680, also appears in entries of 1701 and 1703 (Cowper 1897). At some point prior to 1711, however, the lease of the forge was transferred to local ironmasters John Machell and William Rawlinson, although the exact date is uncertain.

Blast furnaces and refining forges

The first two blast furnaces to be erected in the region, those at Cunsey and Backbarrow, were established in 1711. The Backbarrow furnace was 'blown in' during the same year, and, as partners of the Backbarrow Company, Machell and Rawlinson already had the lease of Cunsey forge, it was used as a refinery in conjunction with the new blast furnace.

The Cunsey Company was founded by Cheshire ironmasters Daniel Cotton and Edward Hall, who built their furnace on a site close to the outflow of Cunsey Beck to lake Windermere (Fig 1), and was put into blast in 1712. During the following year, the bloomforge at Backbarrow was converted to a finery forge (CRO(B) BZ185). Fell (1908, 247) implies that Cunsey forge was similarly 'rebuilt and newly equipped in 1713', although supporting evidence is slight. Production figures for this period (Table 1), for instance, highlight the significant contribution Cunsey forge made to the region's output of bar iron, and would suggest that it operated throughout 1713.

FORGE	1710	1711	1713
Cunsey	68	36.5	43
Backbarrow	36	12	-
Force	23.5	7.5	26
Hacket	19.5	11.5	-

Table 1 : Production of bar iron in tons. (source: Fell 1908, 252)

In 1715, the Backbarrow Company's lease of Cunsey forge expired, and it passed into the hands of the Cunsey Company, who immediately reconstructed the forge and worked it as a refinery in conjunction with their furnace (Fell 1908, 192).

Raw materials – iron ore

An agreement of March 1694 (LRO DDSa 38/2), between Richard Patrickson, Thomas Addison and Henry Rooper demonstrates the parties' willingness to supply Myles Sandys with iron ore from 'pits in Grasmere or any other pits within their lease nearer to Windermeere water' for use at Cunsey forge. Samples of haematite ore recovered during the excavation are consistent with known occurrences in the Grasmere area (B Young pers comm). Fell, citing the toponymy of 'Great Ore Gate' and 'Little Ore Gate', also postulated the importation of ore to Cunsey from the iron mines in Langdale (1908, 193).

Raw materials – charcoal

An agreement between the Penningtons of Muncaster and William Wright, dated 10 April 1623, refers to the sale of all the oak and timber trees at Hacket Ground in Little Langdale for £250 (*op cit*, 191). It is presumed that this was aimed at securing an ample supply of charcoal for use at Cunsey forge (Bowden 2000, 68), although it seems likely that this supply would have terminated with the construction of Hacket forge in 1630.

A later document, dated to 27 January 1701, refers to William Brathwayte of Bryars in Sawrey Extra agreeing to supply Myles Sandys '50 waynloads of charcoal yearly at Consey forge, for 19s a load if iron sells at less than £15 a ton, and 20s if iron sells at £16 a ton or more' (LRO DDSa 2/18). The species of timber are not specified, and whilst the results of an excavation at the Muncaster Head ironworking site concluded that oak accounted for 70% of the wood used (Tylecote and Cherry 1970, 97), preliminary analysis of charcoal samples recovered from Cunsey forge identified alder or hazel, and ash or oak.

Protracted closure

Upon the expiry of the Cunsey Company's lease in 1750, their collateral is thought to have passed to the Backbarrow

Company, and that neither Cunsey furnace nor forge worked after this date (Fell 1908, 193). However, an inventory of stock (LRO DDSa 2/26) and an inventory of goods (LRO DDSa 2/27) at Cunsey forge, compiled on 16 October 1757, demonstrates that the forge was equipped with three forge anvils, nine forge hammers, numerous plates, and an assortment of forge tools. Interestingly, a list of 'Smithy Tools' is itemised separately, and these include an anvil, bellows, files, stamps, and punches. The comprehensive inventory of goods, seemingly complied in advance of their sale, mentions the 'chafery, lower fynery, and upper fynery with all appurtenances'. Similarly, Awty (1964, 20) reassessed the evidence cited by Fell, and concluded that Cunsey forge may not have been transferred to the Backbarrow Company until 1762.

In 1818, the Backbarrow Company was bought out by Harrison, Ainslie and Company who, in 1824, inherited the Cunsey site as part of the Backbarrow Company's concerns (Fell 1908, 209). The absence of Cunsey forge from Christopher Greenwood's 'Map of the County Palatine of Lancaster' (1818), suggests that little remained of the site for Harrison, Ainslie and Company to inherit, and Fell noted that the Backbarrow Company 'had to pay a considerable sum for dilapidations' (*ibid*).

Later developments

Commercial trade directories provide little information of the 19th and 20th century history of the site. The only entry of relevance is contained within a directory of 1911, which lists William Brockbank as a wood hoop maker, and gives his address as the 'Old Forge, Cunsey' (Bulmer 1911, 343-4). However, Brockbank's enterprise was perhaps short-lived, as his business does not appear in subsequent trade directories.

The census returns, and particularly those for 1871 (LRO RG10/4247), provide some additional details. These state that Cunsey forge was occupied in 1871 by John Askew, his wife Catherine, and their son John. The Askews are recorded as 'labourers', suggesting that the forge was not used for industrial purposes. A separate entry, that of Margaret Jackson, is also credited as residing at the 'Old Forge'.

Since the 1950s, the surviving buildings were used for agricultural purposes, until their partial demolition during the mid-1980s (D Walker pers comm).

SITE DESCRIPTION

The visible surface features pertaining to the forge complex incorporate an area of slightly less than one hectare, which concurs with the two acres mentioned in the lease of 1621. In spatial terms, the site is dissected into two main components by a trackway that runs broadly NE/SW between Cunsey Bridge and Eel House. On the SW edge of the track lies a linear range of stone buildings, aligned parallel to the track for a distance of some 47m. The archaeological investigation was focused on two adjoining stone buildings in the centre of the range (Fig 2), whilst immediately contiguous to the NW are two smaller buildings, which are cut into a terrace at a slightly higher level. These have been interpreted as an office (Bowden 2000).

Situated to the SW are the vegetation-infested remains of another large stone building, some 16.94m long (Fig 2). The south wall of this building survives extant, but other elements were demolished some time ago (D Walker pers comm). The surviving wall does not contain either windows or doors, suggesting it to represent the remnants of the charcoal barn, although there is no charcoal staining visible on either the walls or the stone slab floor. Several floor slabs had been removed, exposing a concentrated deposit of

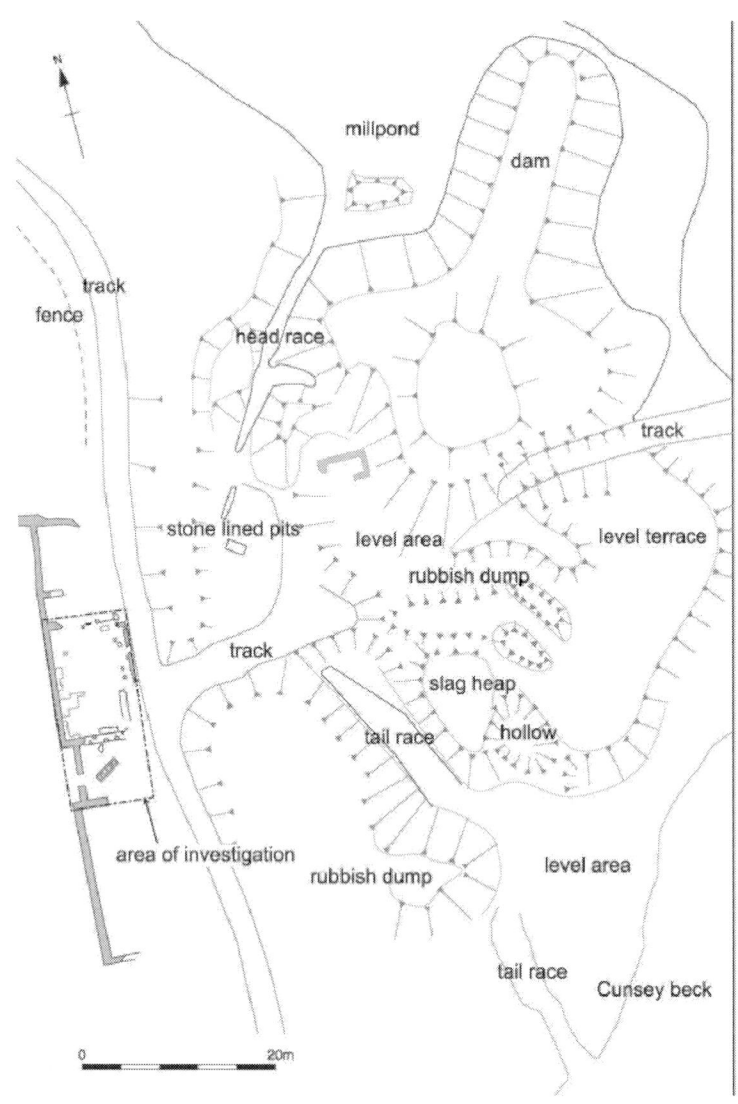

Fig.2 Site plan, showing area of investigation

ironworking residues; this was not investigated archaeologically, although a small sample was collected for metallurgical assessment.

The surviving remains to the NE of the track provide substantial evidence for ironworking, and are likely to represent the focus of such activity. In order to place the excavated part of the site in its context as a component of the entire ironworking complex, a summary description of this area is useful.

The N extent of the complex is marked by a large depression, which represents the former millpond. The E edge of the millpond is retained by a 2m high dam across the valley floor from the S edge of Cunsey Beck; it is presumed that the 'floodgates' mentioned in an indenture of 1647 (CRO(B) BD/HJ/89/8) would have been fitted to the dam to regulate the flow of the beck. A well-constructed stone wall, some 7m in length, at the N terminus of the dam may have been associated with such a structure.

A rock-cut channel at the S edge of the millpond was probably the head race to the forge (Fig 2). A short section of the channel is lined with a stone wall, which incorporates several hearth bottoms, or '*mossers*', in its build. The head race terminates close to a rectangular stone-lined pit, measuring some 3.5m long, whilst a second stone-lined pit lies a short distance to the S. Both structures are currently partially obscured by modern dumping, although it is tempting to interpret them as wheelpits. The remnants of another rectangular stone structure lies to the N, the function of which remains unclear.

A water channel that emerges from beneath the modern track, and continues along an SE direction to join with

Cunsey Beck (Fig 2), almost certainly represents the tail race from the forge.

The area to the E is dominated by massive slag tips, which extend SE parallel to the beck for a distance of at least 50m. The tips include numerous hearth bottoms, providing testimony to the considerable amount of ironworking undertaken on the site. The slag tips are bounded to the N by a trackway that leads to the beck. Its position corresponds to a ford shown on the first edition 1:10,560 Ordnance Survey map of 1851.

PROJECT BACKGROUND

During the 1980s, the surviving elements of the forge (Fig 3) were largely demolished, leaving only a few walls standing. In June 2002, the Lake District National Park Authority Archaeology Service was notified that these fragmentary

Fig.3 The principal building and adjacent structure in the 1980s, prior to their demolition (courtesy of Mike Davies-Shiel)

remains had sustained further demolition; the end wall and part of the rear wall of the building had been demolished, and the floor had been substantially disturbed, revealing various features of archaeological significance including areas of *in situ* concreted metal-working waste.

A programme of archaeological investigation was thus proposed, which, in the short term, was designed to examine and record the features and deposits exposed within the damaged structure, and included a limited programme of geophysical survey. In the medium term, the consolidation of the remains of the structure was anticipated, and the burying of the exposed deposits beneath a geotextile layer. It was also proposed to record the remainder of the site via topographical and geophysical surveys, and to develop a management programme for the longer term.

THE EXCAVATION

Introduction

The excavation comprised two main elements: the general clearance and manual cleaning of the site, followed by the excavation of two trenches within the footprint of the largest, or principal, building (Fig 4).

In the following narrative, a broad phasing has been allocated to the archaeological activity identified in the field. This phasing equates to major events in the evolution of the site, and is based on general stratigraphic trends and provisional finds dating; the results presented here will be refined in the light of further detailed analysis.

Phase 1: The Bloomery/bloomsmithy?

Pending further detailed analysis, there is some evidence for a bloomery/bloomsmithy to have occupied the site,

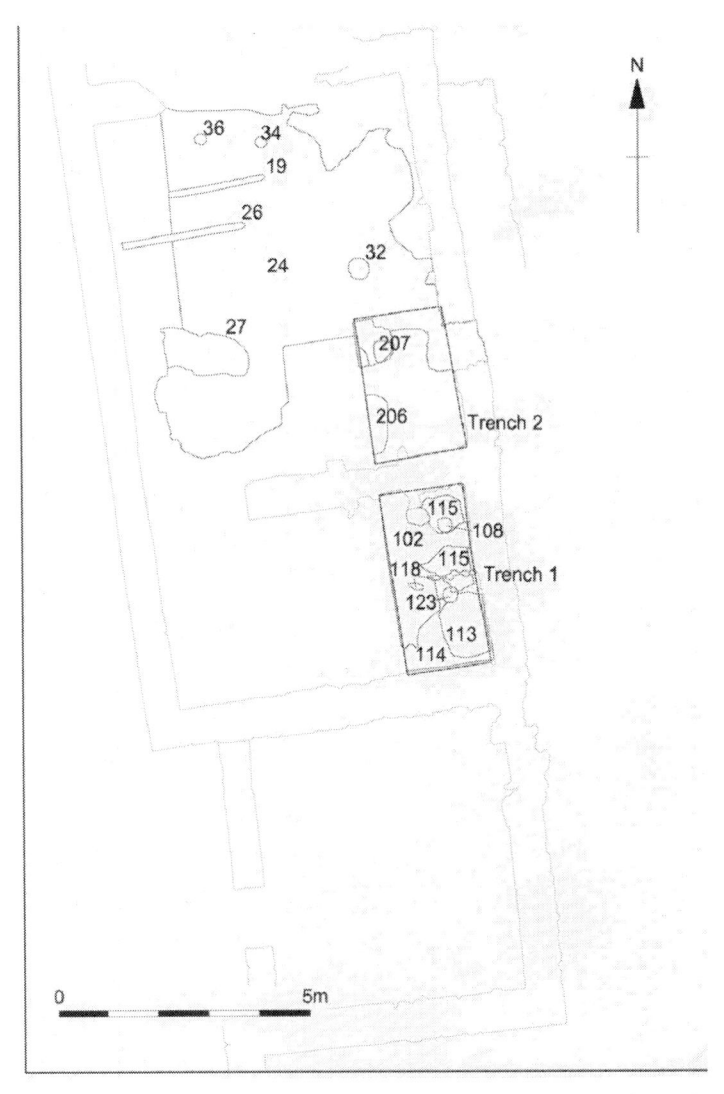

Fig.4 Archaeological evidence for phase 2: the bloomforge

presumably during the late medieval period. This evidence was drawn from an archaeological layer that contained a large proportion of ironworking residues, which have been provisionally identified as bloomery slag. This layer was exposed below the floor level of the iron ore store, whilst similar residues were observed to underlie the floor of the putative charcoal barn, although this area was not formally investigated.

Additionally, the geophysical survey identified a marked dipolar anomaly, tentatively marking the position of a bloomery furnace, beneath a cobble surface (*06*) immediately outside of the building, whilst informal magnetic scanning suggested that similar anomalies may exist on the other side of the track at a point *c* 30m to the SE (Brooks 2003).

Phase 2: The Bloomforge (c 1618 - 1715)

Structural evidence for activity associated with the bloomforge within the W part of the site was seemingly represented by two parallel linear features (*19* and *26*) and two shallow postholes (*34* and *36*). Excavation of the linear features revealed them to have vertical sides and flat bases, aiding their interpretation as timber cill beams for an insubstantial structure. The W terminus of feature *19* correlated with the distinct, linear W extent of a widespread layer (*24*), hinting at the position of a partition at right angles to *19* (Fig 4). Postholes *34* and *36* lay to the N.

A larger posthole (*32*) lay to the SE, and was perhaps associated with a deposit of compact, burnt clay (*207*), which was exposed a short distance to the S within Trench 2 (Fig 4). It is suggested that clay *207* represented the vestiges of a hearth, and posthole *32* marked the position of an item of forge equipment, such as a small anvil. Evidence for ironworking within this part of the site was provided by several deposits, including charcoal-rich lens *27* and layer *24*, which contained abundant nodules of iron slag and yielded a coin of William III dated to AD 1695-99.

Within Trench 1, a spread of compact, burnt clay (*113*) was interpreted as the remnants of another hearth (Fig 4). This appeared to be associated with a large posthole (*123*) that contained numerous large stones, indicative of disturbed post-packing material. A similar posthole (*108*) lay to the N, the fill of which yielded fragments of pottery dated to the late 17th or early 18th century. Situated between postholes *123* and *108* was a series of large, flat stones (*118*) placed vertically into the subsoil forming an E/W alignment. It is suggested that these features all represented elements of forge equipment.

Evidence for ironworking within this part of the site was provided by layers *102*, *114* and *115*, which all contained charcoal and nodules of iron slag. Additionally, a farthing of Charles II (1670-80) was recovered from layer *114*.

Phase 3: Refining Forge (c 1715 - 62)

A significant stage in the development of the site was the construction of the stone buildings (Fig 5), perhaps intended to replace insubstantial structures associated with the bloomforge. The principal building had internal dimensions of 11.5m by 6.5m, whilst the adjacent structure measured *c* 8m by 5.5m. Excavation revealed the footings of the external walls of the principal building to have been cut into Phase 2 deposits, whilst a coin retrieved from the fabric of one wall has been dated to 1714, providing corroboration for the documented period of reconstruction of the site undertaken by the Cunsey Company in 1715.

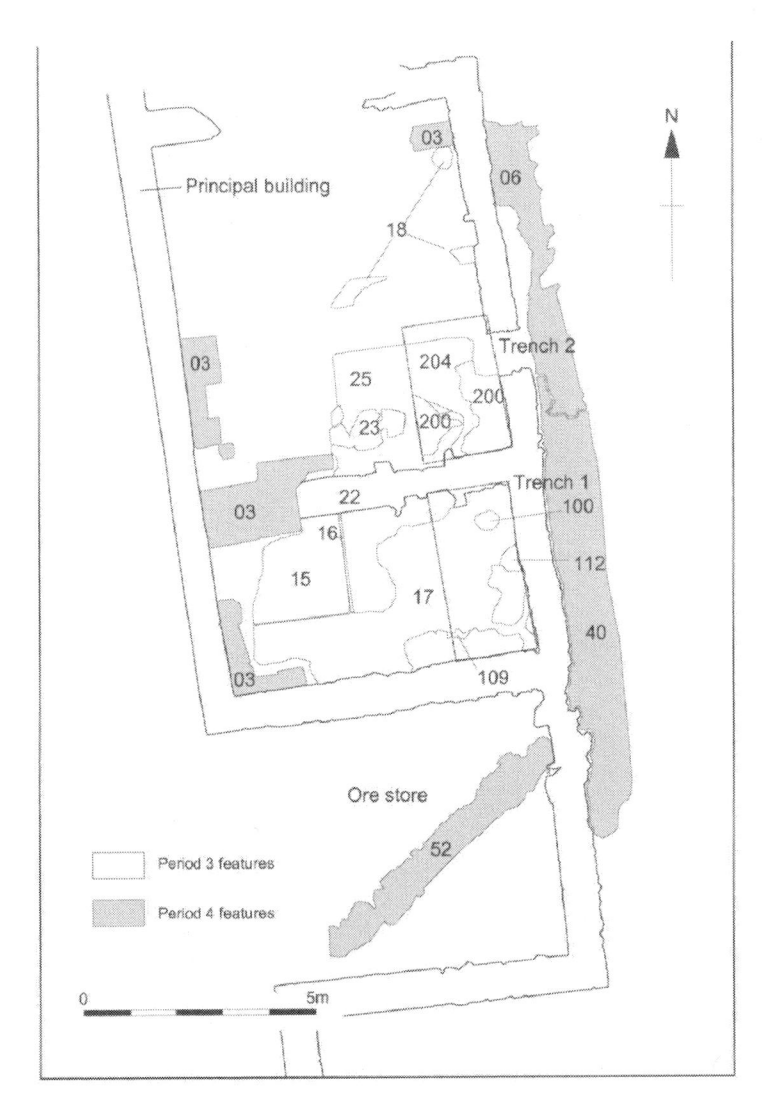

Fig. 5 Archaeological evidence for phase 3: the refining forge.

The principal building was effectively divided into two, broadly equal, components by an internal partition wall (*22*). This wall incorporated a symmetrical feature in its build, the plan form of which was reminiscent of a double-breasted fireplace. However, there was no indication for this structure having been subjected to heat, and the absence of any sooting deposits suggested use as a fireplace to be unlikely. Situated immediately to the N of wall *22* were five, carefully placed, large stone slabs (*23*), the central of which had been heat-affected. The stones had been set onto a rectangular area of compacted clay (*25*), which, in the vicinity of stones *23*, had been discoloured by extreme temperatures. Clay *25* contained dense concentrations of charcoal flecking and ironworking residues in its upper surface, suggesting it to have been a workshop floor. Patches of indurated smithing waste (*18*) that were revealed to the N corroborated this.

Another compacted clay floor (*15*), measuring 2.2m by 2.1m, was revealed to the S of partition wall *22* (Fig 5). The E edge of floor *15* was bounded by the remnants of a timber cill beam (*16*), which presumably marked the position an internal partition. Situated immediately to the E was an extensive layer of indurated smithing waste (*05/100/109*), effectively forming a floor, and associated deposits of industrial detritus, *17* and *103*.

Excavation revealed the adjacent building to contain a 0.20m thick deposit of haematite ore fragments in a matrix of bright reddish-brown clay (*54*), confirming that the building had been used as an ore store.

Phase 4: Late Developments (Post-c1762)

The principal building was modified to accommodate a

change in function, notably by the reduction of the central partition wall (*22*) to its foundation. This, together with smithing waste *05* and other deposits representing ironworking activity, were overlain by a sequence of bedding

Fig. 6 General view of the site during excavation

layers for flagstone floor *03*. The floor had been largely disturbed, but remained *in situ* across the W part of the building (Fig 6). A cobble surface (*06*), which was external to the building and bounded the NE edge of the study area, was seemingly of a contemporary date.

The thick deposit of haematite exposed within the ore store had been cut by a large culvert (*52*), aligned broadly NE/SW across the excavated area. The W wall of the ore store, clearly of a later date to the other walls, may also have been constructed at the same time.

A small range of artefacts, including fragments of window glass and pottery of 19th and early 20th century date, was recovered from a soil horizon (*40*), that was exposed along the front of the building. These seemingly represented domestic activity.

CONCLUSIONS

The archaeological features at the site of Cunsey forge as a whole are substantial and extensive, and provide one of the best surviving examples of a bloomforge/refining forge in the region. Both types of site are comparatively rare, and are generally poorly understood due to lack of research; current definitions of bloomforges and refining forges are based largely on the results of the two separate programmes of excavation at Stony Hazel forge (Davies-Shiel 1970; Cranstone 1985), which have resulted in differing interpretations.

The archaeological investigation has provided a valuable opportunity to examine an element of Cunsey forge that was hitherto considered to be ancillary to ironworking *per se*. However, whilst further fieldwork close to the putative wheel pits may confirm that area to have been the focus of the finery forge, iron was undoubtedly worked within the study area during this period, particularly within the SE part of the building. One possibility is that the excavated area was dedicated to smithing, whilst preceding deposits are likely to represent activity associated with the bloomforge.

ACKNOWLEDGEMENTS

Oxford Archaeology North (OA North) would like to thank John Hodgson, the Lake District National Park Authority Senior Archaeologist, for considerable assistance throughout the course of the project. OA North is also grateful to Mike Davies-Shiel for providing valuable background information, photographs, and encouragement, to Dr Brian Young for advice on the haematite samples, and to David Cranstone who acted as a consultant. Thanks are also expressed to the landowner, Miles Sandys, and to David

Walker of Low Cunsey Farm, for their support and local knowledge.

The Lake District National Park Authority commissioned the project, with funding provided by English Heritage, who are gratefully acknowledged.

BIBLIOGRAPHY

Primary Sources

Greenwood, C, 1818 'Map of the County Palatine of Lancaster'
Ordnance Survey, 1851 First Edition 1:10,560 map
Public Record Office (PRO), London
PL 6/22 Palatine of Lancaster. Chancery Court: Pleadings, Bills, 1685
Cumbria County Record Office (CRO(B)), Barrow
The Furness Collection
BZ185 Day book of the Backbarrow Company, 1711-15
Hart, Jackson and Sons, Ulverston
BD/HJ/89/8 Indenture between William Wright and Rowland ?Lawson, 20 June   1647
Lancashire County Record Office (LRO), Preston
DDSa 2/5 Lease, 2 September 1621
DDSa 2/11 Agreement, 2 May 1639
DDSa 2/18 Agreement, 27 January 1700/1
DDSa 2/26 Inventory of stock at Cunsey Forge, 16 October 1757
DDSa 2/27 Inventory of goods at Cunsey Forge, 16 October 1757
DDSa 38/1 Partnership, 19 October 1681
DDSa 38/2 Agreement, March 1693/4
RG10/4247 Census Returns, 1871

SECONDARY SOURCES

Awty, BG, 1964 Backbarrow and Pennybridge Furnace Accounts,

1763-80, *Trans Lancashire Cheshire Antiq Soc*, **116**, 19-38

Awty, BG, and Phillips, CB, 1980 The Cumbrian Bloomery Forge in the Seventeenth Century and Forge Equipment in the Charcoal Iron Industry, *Trans Newcomen Soc*, **51**, 25-40

Bowden, M, 2000 *Furness Iron: The Physical Remains of the Iron Industry and Related Woodland Industries of Furness and Southern Lakeland*, (Swindon)

Brooks, IP, 2003 Geophysical Survey, Engineering Archaeological Services, unpubl rep

Bulmer, T, 1911 *History, Topography and Directory of Furness and Cartmel*, (Preston)

Cowper, HS (ed), 1897 *The Oldest Register Book of the Parish of Hawkshead in Lancashire, 1568-1704*, (London)

Cranstone, D, 1985 Stony Hazel Forge: Interim Report, unpubl rep

Davies-Shiel, M, 1970 Excavation at Stony Hazel, High Furness, Lake District, 1968-1969: an Interim Report, *Hist Metall*, **4**, 28-32

Fell, A, 1908 *The Early Iron Industry of Furness and District*, (Ulverston)

Phillips, CB, 1977 William Wright: Cumbrian Ironmaster, *Trans Lancashire Cheshire Antiq Soc*, **79**, 34-45

Tylecote, RF, and Cherry, J, 1970 The Seventeenth Century Bloomery at Muncaster Head, *Trans Cumberland Westmorland Antiq Archaeol Soc*, n ser **70**, 69-109

THE BLOOMSMITHIES OF SOUTH WESTMORLAND AND NORTH LANCASHIRE

By Richard Newman

Cumbria County Archaeoologist

The south Westmorland/north Lancashire border area has long been associated with iron making, usually involving the smelting of ores from Furness as the area lacks commercially viable iron ore deposits. This connection only ended with the closure of the Carnforth Ironworks in 1929. Until then there had been a near continuous iron production from at least the medieval period. The bloomsmithy phase in the iron industry in this area focused on the seventeenth century, though it may have commenced in the later sixteenth century and certainly continued on into the eighteenth. What little co-ordinated archaeological research has been undertaken has highlighted issues surrounding the definition of site types and the problems caused by recognition, identification and prioritisation for archaeological curators and potentially for researchers.

The total absence of detailed archaeological research into bloomsmithies in the area, beyond visual observation and site identification, compels anyone studying this topic to rely on the documentary record. These are often misleading as both recent secondary sources and primary contemporary observations are often confused and inaccurate, meaning that much detective work is necessary to find the truth. Even so, the study area inspired an unique and hugely important historical contribution to the understanding of the British bloomsmithy when, in the later seventeenth century, John Sturdie from Lancashire wrote a description of the water-powered bloomery forge at Milnthorpe in Westmorland.

Defining bloomsmithies

There has been much debate concerning terminology describing aspects of the direct smelting iron industry (see Davies-Shiel 1971). Historical terminology has been borrowed and redefined to have a modern precision not intended or conveyed when originally used. Terms such as smithy, forge and even furnace were not precise and to an extent they could be interchangeable. Contemporary commentators may not have been especially knowledgeable of the industry and thus even less rigorous with their labels. In a quest for precision modern scholars have attempted to create an archaeological typology of the different types of direct smelting iron working sites. Hence, Awty and Philips (1982) eschewed historically well used but imprecise terms such as bloomsmithy in favour of bloomery forge, though bloomforge is preferred in more recent publications (e.g. Bowden 2000). Predictably not all agree, Mike Davies-Shiel (MDS) for example argues for the retention of bloomsmithy as a site type but uses bloomforges when ironmongering was also carried out to produce a range of wares (Cumbria SMR). Too much attention to defining typologies, especially when some of the terminology is derived from historical sources can be counterproductive, causing sterile debates, confusion and a mistaken assumption that modern definitions have an historical veracity.

Earlier scholars used a simple typology for the development of the iron industry. Sites that produced wrought iron directly from iron ore were divided between bloomeries, water-powered bloomeries and bloomsmithies (Awty and Phillips 1982, p.25). Terms such as furnace and forge were reserved for the indirect process. This typology is not precise enough to specify every technological variation but it is sufficiently flexible to allow for the inclusion of these variations as subtypes. For example the distinction between low and high-shaft bloomeries fits within the broader category of water-powered bloomery (see Cranstone 2001, p.186). Under this simple but useable typology bloomsmithies used water power to both smelt the ore and to power a tilt hammer to make iron bars, using two wheels, one for each function. Such an ironworks would have one or more hearths. In seventeenth century Cumbria two or three hearths appeared usual, with at least one for smelting the ore and another for reheating the iron to work it into bars (Awty and Phillips 1982). This second hearth could have been used for producing iron goods as well so archaeologically there is no need to distinguish between the bloomsmithy and the so called bloomforge.[1] Whether or not iron wares were produced on a site relates to a difference in the nature of the business, but not necessarily in the character of the structural remains.

Following Awty and Phillips' (1982) assessment of the seventeenth century Cumbrian water-powered bloomery industry, the term bloomsmithy was suppressed in modern terminologies. It rarely appears on the internet, for example, and more worryingly the bloomsmithy does not appear at all in the Royal Commission's *Thesaurus of Monument Types* (2nd edn. 1998). This has considerable implications for both conservation and research. As a consequence of the term not being recognised, this category of site was not evaluated in its own right during the Monuments Protection Programme's review of the quality and significance of surviving iron industry remains. In some areas this type of site was overlooked altogether. Neither the Lancashire nor Cumbria SMRs recognise the site category.

Attempts have been made to define different types of water-powered bloomeries but this has itself caused confusion. To simplify matters the term bloomsmithy and other disputed terms have not been used in SMRs, causing important developmental stages in the direct smelting iron industry to be lost amongst the wider ensemble of bloomery sites. Known sites are not correctly identified and they do not show as a separate monument type when using SMRs to plan future research. Thus the attempt to create a precise terminology has actually led to imprecision and obscures the important fact that bloomsmithies are a unique site type representing a particular developmental phase in the iron industry, a phase well represented by sites in North West England.

Identifying bloomsmithies

Using a list by MDS as a starting point there are three bloomsmithies noted in Westmorland south of Kendal and three in north Lancashire. Not all are noted in the SMRs for the counties. From north to south the first is at Natland. Referenced by MDS as a bloom forge (and thus a producer of iron goods), little is known about the site but it appears to have been in production by the 1730s and to have continued in existence for much of the eighteenth century.

Further south along the River Kent is the site of Force Forge near Sedgwick. This has been claimed by some to be a bloomsmithy originating variously in the late seventeenth century or in 1723. There may be some confusion over references and sources for this site as Alfred Fell confused it with Milnthorpe Forge not far to the south (1908, p.205), and it can also be mistaken for an identically named bloomsmithy at Rusland. The archaeologically identifiable site of Force Forge was definitely in existence by 1763 when it was a finery and chafery forge converting cast iron pigs made at a blast furnace into wrought iron bars and plates (Cumbria SMR). At the time it seems to have been only recently erected. Evidence for the works being a finery and chafery comes from the poet Thomas Gray who in 1769 wrote in his journal concerning the site of *"the calmness and brightness of the evening, the roar of the waters and the thumping of huge hammers at an iron forge not far distant"*. He went on to describe Force Falls *"the stream is much impaired in beauty since the forge was erected. I went on down to the forge (from which proceeded the din described) and saw the demons at work by the light of their own fires. The iron is brought in pigs to Millthrop by sea from Scotland etc., and here is beat into bars and plates"* (Fell 1908, p.205; Somervell 1930, p.73). Nicholson and Burn's county history of 1777 confirms the function and recent origin of the forge: *"on the west side of the Force was erected some few years ago by Thos. Holme Esq & other gentlemen in Kendal, a forge for beating out pigs of iron and other iron work, which employs several families who have dwelling houses and offices near adjoining"*. (p.208). It is generally considered that Force Forge was built on the site of the medieval corn mill known as Under Levens Mill (Somervell 1930, p.73), but it is possible that the grist mill site was initially converted for use as a bloomsmithy before becoming a finery and chafery forge.

Milnthorpe Forge on the River Bela was undoubtedly a bloomsmithy, as its nature and function were described in 1675 as well as in contemporary documents (Awty and Phillips 1982, p.25). It is possible that the bloomsmithy was built by William Wright, a well known bloomsmith in Lancashire-over-Sands, who moved to Milnthorpe in 1650

(Phillips 1977, p.20). His son, Balthazar Wright, seems to have been the bloomer there from the mid 1650s until his death in 1688 (Phillips 1977, p.27). It seems likely that this event led to the closure of the bloomsmithy for in 1692 Thomas Machel wrote that in Milnthorpe, *"a little above the bridge is a paper mill, formerly an iron forge"* (Ewbank 1963, p.55). As the location of the paper works is known the site of the forge should be easily identifiable, but this is not the case and there have been considerable differences in opinion as to its precise location. Somervell located the forge close to the then gasworks, now an electricity substation. More recently Roger Bingham, whilst broadly favouring Somervell's view, speculated that the forge was situated close to the site of the Bridge End Smithy, a later blacksmiths (1987, p.39). Marshall and Davies-Shiel in their *Industrial Archaeology of the Lake Counties* state that the site of the forge later became a cotton mill and then a paper mill (1969, p.254). Combined documentary study and visual inspection of the river bank has enabled the sequence of enterprises and a more precise location of the forge to be identified.

The paper mill mentioned by Machell in 1692 was by 1777 occupied by two paper mills (Nicolson and Burn, p.201). These two paper mills in 1811 were said to be on the site of a cotton mill and on the site of a forge (Hodgson 1811, p.224). Two paper mills were again mentioned in 1829, though on Mount's map of Milnthorpe in 1826 only one mill is marked (CRO WD/D/Acc.950/49). By 1860 there was only one paper mill and a little upstream from it in that year the gasworks were established (Whellan, p.831). Late eighteenth century documents indicate that the two paper mills were actually under one roof (Bingham 1987, p.157) and it is clear that in 1826 the site was a complex of buildings which could and did from time to time house more than one paper making business. Since the cotton mill referred to as having burnt down in 1816 appears to have lain a little upstream from the paper mills, the description of the paper mills as being on the site of the cotton mill and forge need not be taken too literally, referring to the area where these enterprises were undertaken rather than the precise structure within which they were housed. Erosion by the River Bela in the past couple of decades of a mounded part of the river bank, upstream of the paper mills and later gasworks, has revealed fragments of iron slag and larger concretions of slag and hearth material. This seems to represent the remains of Milnthorpe Forge or at least those of its slag bank. As this site may lie away from any later development it is possible that there is a more significant survival of buried remains than had been previously supposed (Price 1983, p.47).

South from Milnthorpe the next bloomsmithy is on the River Keer, at Keerholme. on the Westmorland/Lancashire border. The forge was owned by William Marshall and seems to have been in smelt between about 1690 and 1720, though MDS has proposed that it was in existence by 1625 (Cumbria SMR). The bloomery slag noticed in the stream bed suggests that it was a bloomsmithy. The greatest concentration of ironworks of all periods and types in the area, however, appears to be in the Lune valley where much work remains to be done both in the field and in searching the archives. A bloomsmithy has been claimed at Hornby, but unless documents contained at Hornby Castle indicate differently, recent work on the Lancashire Extensive Urban Survey would indicate that the possible site next to Hornby Bridge was only a blacksmith's workshop (Egerton Lea 2003). It is possible that it was a blacksmiths from at least the late sixteenth century (Chippindall 1939, pp.32-3). The owner of the reputed bloomsmithy at Hornby in the early seventeenth century was Lord Morley and Mounteagle of Hornby Castle, who was said to have established ironworks within his lordship (PRO C10/39/123; Awty and Phillips 1982, p.39), an area which in the early 17th century the lordship included the manor of Tatham (Farrer and Brownbill 1914, p.195). Further up the River Hindburn from Hornby, at Birks Farm, Tatham and 140m upstream from Furnace Ford Bridge, deposits of scoria were found towards the end of the nineteenth century. The situation of such a site adjacent to a stream clearly indicates that it was a bloomsmithy (Lancashire SMR). The apparent lack of documentary evidence and the fact that nothing was remembered of the site at the time of its discovery would suggest that it had probably existed in the earlier 17th century and was possibly one of the ironworks set up by Lord Morley and Mounteagle. MDS also records a bloomsmithy at Caton (Cumbria SMR). The only forge known recorded at Caton in the 18th century was on the banks of the Artle Beck in 1727, a finery and chafery forge (Price 1983, p.49). By the 1750s this was part of the Halton Iron Company which also owned a blast furnace and forge at Halton and Leighton Beck blast furnace. Clearly at the time it was not a bloomsmithy but a forge producing bar iron from pig iron produced at Leighton and Halton.

One other Lancashire site should be mentioned with this group, a recorded bloomsmithy at Garstang. Schubert references this site as having been observed in Bishop Pococke's travelogue in which, on passing through Garstang in 1756, he observed *"the smoke from some smelting houses, which are erected there"* (1957, p.152). In the 1780s Lewis in his treatise on iron manufacturing described the process of providing the blast to the hearth via the water driven bellows at Garstang and his diagram was reproduced by Schubert (1957, 151). In spite of such conclusive references no site has been positively identified, even during the recent review of the town's archaeological remains as part of the Lancashire Extensive Urban Survey (Egerton Lea 2002). A year before Pococke's visit, the Swedish traveller Angerstien commented on the presence of blacksmith's shops producing iron wares in Garstang and on a bloomery six miles to the west (Berg 2001, p.293). This seems unlikely to be the bloomery seen by Pococke but Angerstien's account was only third hand. He also referred to another bloomery a few miles away called 'Mihltarp'. Angerstien's editors were unable to locate this but it is likely to be a reference to Milnthorpe, the site of a bloomsmithy that ceased operations 65 years before Angerstien's visit! All that can be inferred from Angerstien's and Pococke's accounts is that there was a bloomsmithy associated with Garstang and that the smoke from it could be seen when passing through the town. There is a well known finery forge in the neighbouring township of Barnacre to the east, part of the parish of Garstang. This listed building is a 19th century structure known to be on the site of an 18th century forge (Lancashire SMR). The smoke from such a forge would be visible to travellers passing through Garstang. It seems likely that Barnacre forge may be on the site of and was the successor to the Garstang bloomsmithy. A possible bloomery site in Garstang has recently been discovered by Oxford Archaeology North, however and may offer an alternative location (pers comm. Ian Miller).

Milnthorpe forge

Two letters by John Sturdie about Lancashire iron production, published in the *Philosophical Transactions* in 1693-4 and later quoted by both Fell and Schubert, contain details of the operation of Milnthorpe Forge. They are invaluable as the only contemporary account of the bloomsmithing process. *"It is very much like a common blacksmiths, viz., a plain open hearth or bottom without any enclosing walls, only where the nose of the bellows come through a wall there is a hollow place (which they call the furnace) made of iron plates, as is also that part of the hearth next adjoining. This hollow place they fill and up-heap with charcoal, and lay the ore (broken small) all round about the charcoal upon the flat hearth, to bake it, as it were, or neal and thrust it in by little and little into the hollow, where it is melted by the blast. The glassie scoriae run very thin, but the metal is never in perfect fusion, but settles as it were in a clod, that they take out with tongs, and turn it under great hammers, which at the same time beat off (especially at first taking out of the furnace) a deal of coarser scoriae, and form it after several heats into bars. They use no limestone to promote the flux, for that I enquired particularly"*. The lack of enclosing walls has been taken to indicate that the Milnthorpe forge would be very similar illustrated sixteenth century European examples. These appear to have had three open sides (Schubert 1957). It is unclear, nevertheless, as to whether the description applies to the building within which the hearth was situated or is simply a description of an open hearth.

The reliability of Sturdie's description and the validity of comparing Milnthorpe with sixteenth century bloomsmithies in central Europe, as Schubert did (1957, pp149-51) was challenged by Awty and Phillips (1982). They said that an interpretation based on Sturdie's text led to an over-simplification of the nature of 17th century bloomeries. They contended, on the basis of contemporary documentary records and archaeological evidence from Muncaster Head, that they were similar in equipment and appearance to 17th century finery and chafery forges. The apparent contradiction between Sturdie's account and other evidence may be due to a lack of clarity rather than unreliability, leading to inaccurate interpretations of its meaning. If Sturdie's reference to the bloomsmithy being like a common blacksmith's refers to the nature of the smelt hearth rather than implying that the ironworks was like a blacksmith's workshop, then it is almost certainly accurate. Equally too much can be read into Sturdie's statement that the iron was beaten into bars in the same furnace in which it was smelted.

The post-medieval direct process used at least two hearths, one for producing the smelt and the other to reheat the smelt to beat it into bars. By the 17th century the second hearth was routinely referred to as a chafery and in 1671 reference is made to the chafery bellows at Milnthorpe (Awty and Philips 1982, p29). It is possible, given the imprecision of the language used by Sturdie and his contemporaries, that he was referring to the bloomsmithy as a furnace rather than a particular hearth. In such circumstances Sturdie was merely drawing a distinction between the bloomery method of working and that of the indirect process.

Another aspect of Milnthorpe forge's operation that is disputed is the possibility that peat was used there as a fuel. Local manorial documents contain repeated prohibitions against the operators taking peat from the mosses. Morton considered that peat was not used at Milnthorpe (1965, 423-4). Sturdie, an advocate of peat use, did not mention it at Milnthorpe, John Lucas in his 1720s history of Warton, stated categorically that charcoal was the only fuel used (Ford and Fuller-Maitland 1931, 59), but comments cannot be relied on as he was comparing the products of Leighton Beck blast furnace with those of Milnthorpe forge. He said that the product from Leighton, which famously did use peat, was superior to that of the former Milnthorpe forge - however he was comparing blast furnace pig iron with bloomsmithy bar iron, something of a pointless debate. Colin

Phillips argues that the 'prohibited' peat was used for building purposes (1977, 21), as noted at other North-West ironworks. However, this would have used so little peat that it would hardly have merited manorial regulations to discourage it.

The distribution of bloomsmithies

The distribution of bloomsmithies differed from that of bloomeries primarily because of their reliance on water power, though they also required areas of either managed or underexploited woodland for fuel. Local availability of iron ore seems not to have been a dominating factor which is why, as Colin Phillips noted, there is a similar density of important smelt sites in iron-poor south Westmorland as in iron-rich Furness. The coastal shipping around Morecambe Bay distributed the raw materials and presumably helped move the finished products.[2] Without adequate coastal transport it is doubtful that north Lancashire would have sustained its iron industry. The locations of the bloomsmithies thus seem to have been conditioned by ready availability of fuel and water. These factors also influenced the distribution of charcoal blast furnaces and their attendant forges and thus the Westmorland/Lancashire border district continued to be a focus of iron manufacturing long after the disappearance of the bloomsmithy.

A further factor which encouraged the later development of an area from bloomsmithies to blast furnaces was labour. Bloomsmithies had encouraged skills in mechanised ironworking and woodland management. Not surprisingly later manufacturers were eager to use what they could of these skills, which could well be among the reasons some bloomsmithies were developed into finery forges

Significance, future research and conservation

The bloomsmithy can be demonstrated to be a definable and important stage in the evolution of the iron industry, at least in North-West England. It dominated the iron industry of much of the region in the seventeenth century and not just in Furness as is often claimed (Cranstone 2001, 188). It lasted as long as the charcoal-fueled blast furnace, and exercised some influence over the development of that later phase. Yet in a recent publication purporting to be a review of 'the archaeology of the wrought iron industry in North West England', a total of four lines are devoted to this phase of development (Nevell and Roberts 2003, 5). It does however reiterate David Crossley's statement from 1992 that very few water-powered bloomery sites have been archaeologically investigated (21-2). A similar lack of coverage exists in English Heritage's review of the Furness iron industry, though a summary of the archaeological work carried out at the water-powered bloomery at Muncaster Head is provided (Bowden 2000, 40; 45-7). The North-West has the best surviving documentary evidence for bloomsmithies in Britain and thus their study and conservation should be seen as a regional priority. This will be difficult to achieve as their existence is not recognised by official archaeological terminology. Especial importance should be placed on confirming the site location of Milnthorpe forge and assessing the nature of its remains. It should be possible to place this site in a wider context as not only does it have significant documentary evidence relating to it but the investigation of its character can be guided by the results of the recent archaeological work at Cunsey forge (this volume). Both sites appear to have been established by William Wright, so there should be close parallels. Only through such work can conservation priorities for these sites be defined.

The bloomsmithy is perhaps the victim of inadvertent archaeological apartheid. If the site type is not defined then the sites will not be recognised and thus they cannot be prioritised for research. Without research they will not be understood, appreciated and conserved. Beyond the argument over terminology, the lack of attention paid to bloomsmithies to an extent encapsulates the response to many aspects of early post-medieval archaeology in North-West England. All too often we concentrate on the monument types of the early Industrial Revolution, but we neglect those sites that pre-dated them. Sites that were so often the pioneers, that represent processes and developments without which later industrial activity may not have happened. The documentary record of these sites is seldom good and archaeologically they can be difficult to recognise, are often obscured by later activities and consequently remain inadequately understood.

Notes.
1. It is likely that where ironmongering was practiced different hammerscale residues would be found to sites where only bar iron was produced.
2. It is worth noting that because of land carriage costs iron ore was more expensive at Rusland, on the edge of Furness mining district, than it was at Milnthorpe (Awty and Philips 1982, 27)

Reference
CRO WD/D/Acc.950/49   Mount's map of Milnthorpe
PRO C10/39/123

Awty BG and Phillips CB 1982, 'The Cumbrian bloomery forge in the seventeenth century and forge equipment in the charcoal iron industry', *Transactions of the Newcomen Society* **51**, 25-40
Berg T and P (translators) 2001, *R R Angerstien's Illustrated*

Travel Diary 1753-1755 (London: Science Museum)
Bingham RK 1987, *The Chronicles of Milnthorpe* (Milnthorpe)
Bowden M (ed) 2000, *Furness Iron* (English Heritage: Swindon)
Chippindall WH 1939, *A Sixteenth Century Survey and Years Accounts of the Estates of Hornby Castle, Lancashire* (Manchester: Chetham Society **102**)
Cranstone D 2001, Industrial Archaeology – manufacturing a new society, in Newman R *The Historical Archaeology of Britain, c 1540-1900* (Stroud)
Crossley D 1990, *Post-Medieval Archaeology in Britain* (Leicester University Press)
Crossley D 1992, The Iron and Steel Industries. Monuments Protection Programme Step 1 Report, unpub report for English Heritage
Davies-Shiel M 1971, 'The terminology of early iron smelting in Lakeland' *Transactions of the Cumberland and Westmorland Antiquarian and Archaeological Society* **71**,
Egerton Lea Consultancy Ltd 2002,Lancashire Extensive Urban Survey: Garstang Archaeological Assessment, unpub report for Lancashire County Council
Egerton Lea Consultancy Ltd 2003,Lancashire Extensive Urban Survey: Hornby Archaeological Assessment, unpub report for Lancashire County Council
Ewbank JM 1963, *Antiquary on Horseback* (Kendal: Cumberland & Westmorland Archaeological & Antiquarian Society Extra Series **19**)
Fell A 1908, *The Early Iron Industry of Furness and District* (Ulverston)
Ford JR and Fuller-Maitland JA 1931 *John Lucas's History of Warton Parish* (Kendal)

Hodgson J Rev 1811, *Topographical and Historical Description of the County of Westmorland* (Kendal)
Marshall J and Davies-Shiel M 1969, *The Industrial Archaeology of the Lake Counties* (Newton Abbot)
Morton GR 1965, The use of peat in the reduction of iron ore' *Iron and Steel* **38.9**, 421-4
Nevell M and Roberts J 2003, *The Park Bridge Ironworks and the Archaeology of the Wrought Iron Industry in North West England,*

1600 to 1900 (Tameside)
Newman R 1999, Iron working and mining enterprises, *Keer to Kent* **38**, 14-15
Nicolson J and Burn R 1777, *The History and Antiquities of the Counties of Westmorland and Cumberland* (London)
Phillips CB 1977a, 'William Wright: Cumbrian Ironmaster', *Transactions of the Lancashire and Cheshire Antiquarian Society* **79**, 34-45
Phillips CB 1977b, 'The Cumbrian iron industry in the seventeenth century', in Chaloner WH and Ratcliffe BM (eds) *Trade and Transport. Essays in economic history in honour of TS Willan* (Manchester University Press)
Price J 1983, *The Industrial Archaeology of the Lune Valley* (Lancaster: Centre for North-west Regional Studies University of Lancaster Occasional Paper **13**)
Royal Commission on Historical Monuments in England (2nd edn) 1998, *Thesaurus of Monument Types* (Swindon)
Schubert HR 1957, *History of the British Iron and Steel Industry* (London)
Somervell J 1930, *Water-Power Mills of South Westmorland on the Kent, Bela and Gilpin and their Tributaries* (Kendal)

Whellan W 1860, *The History and Topography of the Counties of Cumberland and Westmoreland* (Pontefract)

WILSON HOUSE, LINDALE: JOHN WILKINSON'S PEAT-FUELLED BLAST FURNACE

By David Cranstone

Introduction

Wilson House, Cumbria (SD 426 810) lies on the south side of the Lindale-Kendal road, in the modern civil parish of Upper Allithwaite (formerly a township of Cartmel parish), and within the Lake District National Park. In its present form, it consists of an extensive complex of farm buildings (some ruinous), occupying a rocky hillock above the reclaimed marshland of the Winster valley; the river Winster flows past the south end of the site (Fig 1).

The site of Wilson House is of potential archaeological interest due to its claimed association with Isaac and John Wilkinson, both important figures in the development of the iron industry, and hence of the Industrial Revolution, in the 18th century. Isaac Wilkinson was responsible for important developments in iron-founding and furnace-blowing technology; he was 'potfounder' (foundry master) at Backbarrow Ironworks from 1735 to 1748, became a partner in Low Wood Ironworks in 1748, but moved to Wales by 1753. His son John Wilkinson became a leading ironmaster and industrialist, playing an important role in the development of both the iron industry and the steam engine. His main ironworks were in the Black Country, Shropshire, and North Wales, but he retained interests in Cumbria including a home at Castle Head, Lindale (where he was buried in 1808).

Stockdale, the leading 19th century historian of the Cartmel

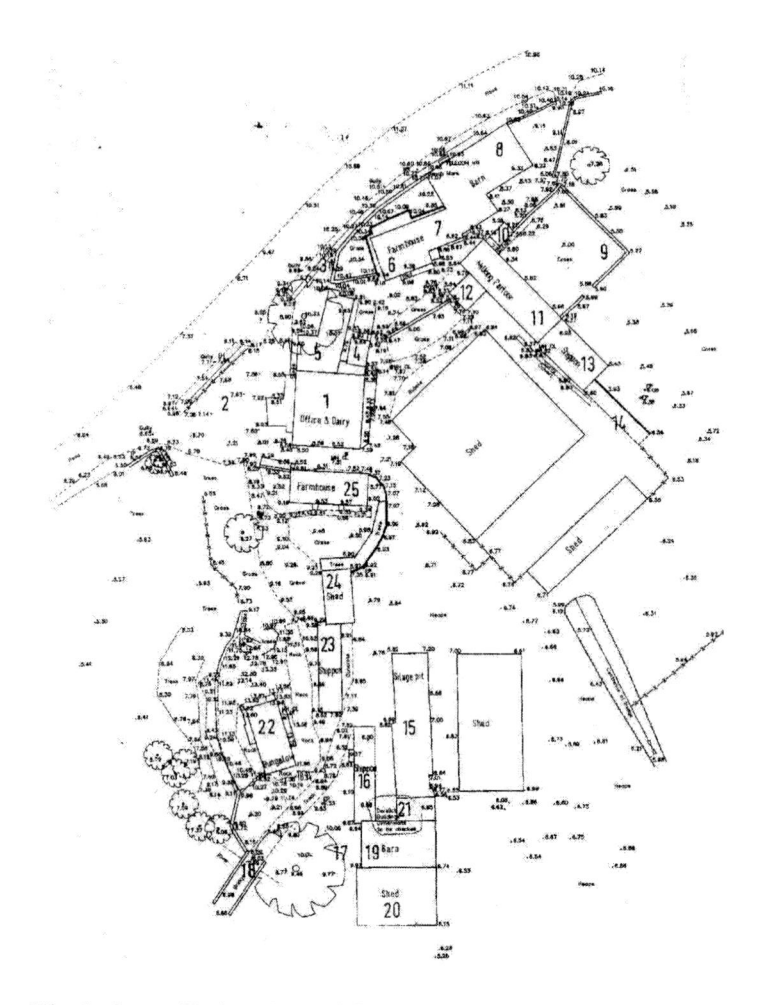

Fig 1. Overall site plan with gazetteer context numbers.

area and a relative of the Wilkinsons, claimed that Isaac Wilkinson set up a blast furnace at Wilson House in 1748 (Stockdale 1872, 210-212), and experimented with peat smelting and iron boats. Recent work by the present author (Cranstone 1991) had indicated that other claims by

Stockdale relating to Isaac Wilkinson were unreliable, and had cast doubt on the existence of a furnace at Wilson House. However, it was understood that references to Wilson House occurred in the Wilkinson correspondence in the Boulton & Watt papers (now in Birmingham Reference Library), and this plus the existence of cast iron pipes with Wilkinson's name cast-in indicated that the Wilkinsons did have some connection with Wilson House.

In 2002, a planning application by the owners of the site resulted in a requirement by the National Park Authority for a 'desk-top assessment' of the historical and field evidence, in order to ascertain the nature of Isaac and/or John Wilkinson's activities (if any) at Wilson House, and the potential for above- or below-ground archaeological remains (Cranstone 2002).

The Historical Evidence

The following programme of primary documentary research was undertaken:

1   Consultation of general and iron-industry records in Cumbria Record Office (CRO), Barrow-in-Furness, Kendal, Carlisle and Whitehaven, and Lancashire Record Office (LRO), Preston. Since preliminary enquiries did not identify any relevant material in Barrow, Carlisle, or Whitehaven, detailed research was confined to Kendal and Preston.

2   Examination of the published volume of Boulton & Watt correspondence, and catalogues for the unpublished collection in Birmingham Reference Library, with selective examination of original documents identified as referring to Wilson House.

3   Correspondence check with other record repositories

known to hold Wilkinson papers (Warrington Public Library, Denbighshire and Flintshire Record Offices and the National Library of Wales). Since these enqiries produced negative results, the repositories were not visited; it is now suspected that some of the negatives were 'false', with information on Wilson House likely to be contained within surveys of the Castle Head estate of which it later formed a part.

'Building numbers' in this section relate to the site gazetteer (below).

Local historical sources

The Lindale parish registers (CRO Kendal WPR99/1) were briefly examined for the 1770s and 1780s; they indicate that occupants of Wilson House included a Robert Ripper in 1778, Edward Mullard in 1782 and 1784, and James Bell in 1787. However, no occupations are stated, so no connection to industrial activity at the site can be made. The register also includes Land Tax Assessments for Upper Allithwaite for 1743, 1746, and 1768. The 1746 assessment shows a Mr Wilkinson paying 4s 9d, and the 1768 assessment a Mr Wilkinson paying 5s 2d (the same amount as in the 1782 assessments below, and therefore probably relating to Wilson House), but the abode is not stated, and other non-relevant Wilkinsons also lived in the area. The only evidence for Isaac Wilkinson's presence at Wilson House therefore remains two documents quoted by Stockdale (1872, 212-3) and not known to survive; an iron ore purchase of 1750 by 'Isaac Wilkinson of Wilson House', and an incroachment on the commons in 1757 by 'Isaac Wilkinson, Bersham, for an incroachment at Wilson House'. Since Wilkinson was probably still a partner in Low Wood furnace in 1750

(Cranstone 1991, 89-90), the former does not form evidence for an ironworks at Wilson House, though the documents (assuming they are correctly transcribed by Stockdale) do confirm that Isaac Wilkinson had property at the site.

Correspondence from John Wilkinson to James Stockdale of Cark (the grandfather of the historian, and a merchant who had various dealings with Wilkinson) survives between 1778 and 1795 (LRO: DDHj acc 1372 Box 2) and contains occasional references to Wilson House, only three of which may relate to an ironworks: on December 23rd 1778 'I have wrote to Mr Dixon of Newlands to ship 40 or 50 tons of Pigs ... by way of ballast to Chester ... I have no objection to there being a whole loading of pigs if such as I want are ready'; on 10th July 1779 '...I must however endeavor to see what they are doing at Wilson House and Castle Head ...'; and on 25th February 1791 '... It was very right to let him have any Pipes or Castings that lay in store at Wilson House.'. The first of these seems from its context to be better interpreted as a shipment of pig iron bought from Newlands furnace, for use in Wilkinson's foundry at Bersham, and the second is unspecific; the third indicates use as a store, with possibly an implication that any ironworks was disused. In December 1783, Wilkinson was shipping 10 tons of pig iron in from Chepstow for Winder & Co of Crooklands, some being for use at Castlehead. Other references to Wilson House, from 1780 onwards, are in relations to enclosure and marshland reclamation (Wilkinson disputing a high valuation by the Vestry, and declining to take in land opposite Wilson House in protest - this reclamation was therefore presumably of the marshes across the Winster from the site, in the township of Meathop rather than Cartmel), and agricultural use (sheep and lambs to Wilson House in February 1788).

The same box also includes various notes by Stockdale the

historian; it is clear that he used his grandfather's letters in compiling the A*nnales Caermoelenses*. After quoting letters from Wilkinson in 1787 and 1788 (surviving in the correspondence) about his iron boats at Bradley and Willey, he specifically states 'before taking his journey to France he had long before actually succeeded in constructing a diminutive [?] one for the canal at Wilson House in the parish of Cartmel'. The box also includes correspondence from James Watt about the steam engine installed at Cark cotton mill in 1787, with considerable detail.

Land Tax returns for Upper Allithwaite survive from 1781 to 1832, with occasional gaps (LRO: QDL/LN/5); records to 1809 were examined. The 1782 assessment lists 'Mr Wilkinson 5s 2d Do for Castle Head 4s 10d do for Mill 1s 8d'; these assessments continue unchanged to 1785, when 'Do for Agnes Walker's 2s 8d' is added, and 1792 when 'Hodgson's 1s 0d', 'Turner's 1s 8d', 'Benson's 2s 4d', and 'Dixon's 6s 5½d' are added. In 1808 and 1809, the entry is changed to 'Trustees of John Wilkinson Esq', showing that Wilkinson retained ownership until his death.

Cartographic evidence

The earliest known mapping to show the site is Yates' map of Lancashire in 1786 (LRO: DP 179/6). This names Wilson House, with a building to the north and a symbol for 'water mills engines etc' to the south, but does not name any works (whereas Backbarrow and Low Wood Ironworks, and Cark cotton mill, are identified by name). It names 'J Wilkinson Esq' at Castle Head, and 'J Wilkinson's improved moss' to the north of Wilson House (roughly between Wilson Hills and Low Green in modern terms).

The next dated map (Fig 2) is the plan of Upper Allithwaite,

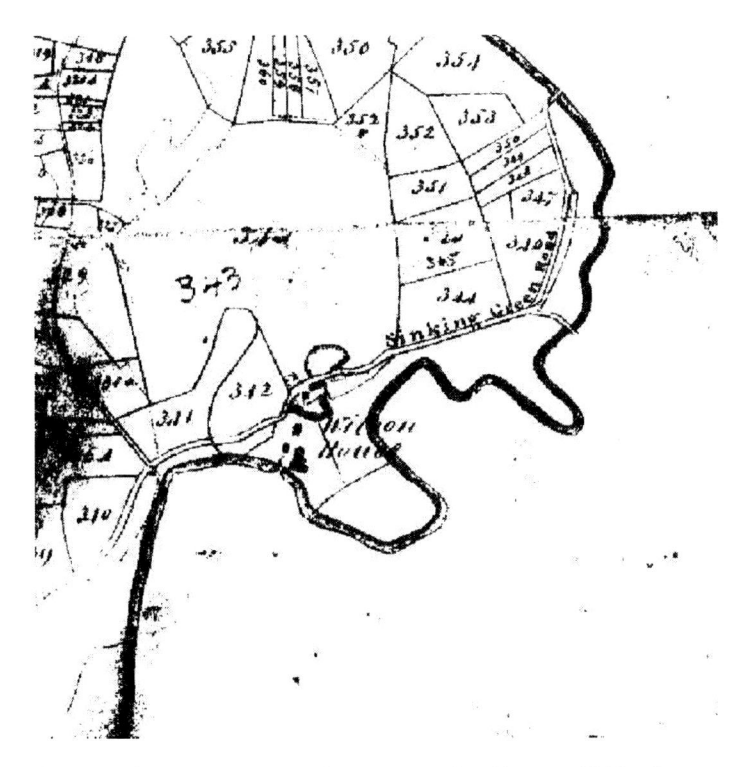

Fig 2. Wilson House as shown on the Cartmell Enclosure Award map (1807) (CRO Kendal: wpr 89/z3)

dated 1807, bound into the Cartmel Enclosure Act (CRO Kendal: WPR 89/Z3); the map and Act also give details of Wilkinson's (surprisingly limited) land allotments within the township. This shows the buildings at Wilson House in moderate detail. However, the site is shown in more detail on two undated maps (CRO Kendal: WPR 89/PR/2716/2) which from their content and annotations must have formed an earlier part of the Enclosure Act process (and are therefore referred to as 'pre-1807' in the ensuing text). The most detailed of these (Fig 3 lower - northwest to the top) shows

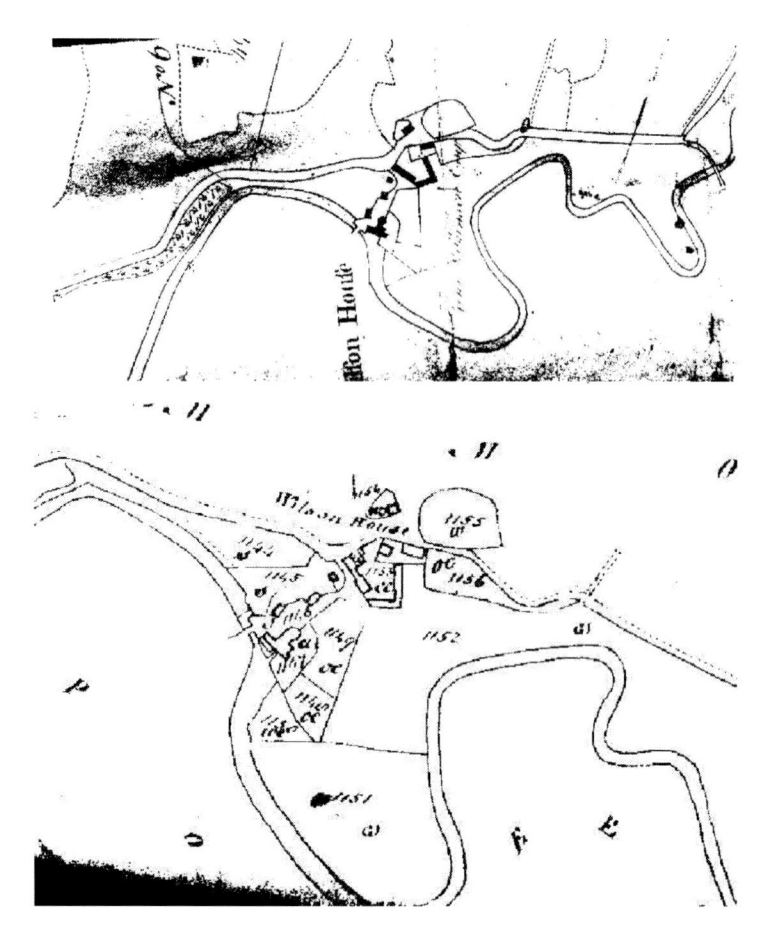

Fig 3. Two maps of Wilson House, pre-1807 (CRO Kendal: WPR 89/PR/2716/2)

buildings 6 and 8 and a distinctive L-shaped range (partly surviving as buildings 11 and 13, see below) on the northern part of the site; a range running west from the southwest end of the L-shaped block may perhaps include building 1 at its west end. To the south of this complex, it depicts the central block of building 25, and a T-shaped group of buildings with a semi-circular extension to the northern limb and a channel from the south side into the Winster, east of the bridge (which is clearly shown); building 22 on Jack Crag and building 24 are also shown. A triangular plot ('1156'), to the east of the northern buildings and faintly shaded on the map, is reminiscent of a millpond in shape, and a similarly-shaded strip ('1157') to the east of Stripes Lane could be interpreted as a fragment of headrace and/or canal. To the west, a probable track between the river bank and plot 1144 may indicate the site of a wharf (see below). A second map in the same deposit (Fig 3 upper) identifies the site as owned by John Wilkinson, but does not show building 6 or the possible building 1 (whose site is covered by the end of a plain rectangular range connecting to the L-shaped range); it may therefore be of earlier date, or a simplification from the first plan.

The next known mapping is the 'proposed' map for the Ulverston and Carnforth Turnpike (undated, but must be c 1818) (LRO: TTK 2). This shows the buildings at small scale, though the L-shaped range is recognisable; only two small buildings are shown in the south part of the site, but in view of the scale and the distance from the proposed road (the modern road to the north of the site) this should not be taken as strong evidence for the destruction of the larger building complex shown on the earlier maps.

Since Tithe maps were never prepared for Cartmel and Upper Allithwaite (LRO, pers. comm.), the next known mapping is the 1st edition 6" OS of 1847 (Lancashire Sheet 13), followed by the first 25" mapping in 1889 (Lancashire Sheet 13/9). The 1847 map (Fig 4) presents considerable problems, since at the south end it shows a group of buildings in the area of 15-21 on a different orientation to both the earlier and the later maps, implying that all the surviving buildings in this area must be of later date. However it shows the L-shaped range as deviating from its orientation on both earlier and later maps, and either omits buildings 6-8 or depicts them as roofless ruins, somewhat distorted in plan. It is therefore suspected that there is a serious metrical distortion in this mapping, possibly connected to its location adjacent to the county boundary (Alastair Oswald, pers. comm.). The L-shaped range has been elongated to the SW from its earlier depictions; this is confirmed by the 1889 mapping.

The 1889 map (Fig 5), by contrast, corresponds well to the surviving form of the buildings, depicting buildings 1, 4, 5, 6 -8, 10-13, 16, 19, 21, 22, 23, 24, and 25, together with various other buildings which do not survive above ground.

Boulton & Watt Papers

This massive collection is in the process of being recatalogued; it is likely to contain further information, but this was not realistically retrievable in advance of full cataloguing. The main sources consulted were:
Boulton and Watt Box 20/2: correspondence from John Wilkinson 1775-1779
Boulton and Watt Portfolio 695b : Drawings
Boulton and Watt B&W 2 : Administrative Letter Book 1777 -1783
James Watt Papers C3/3 : Journal for 1778
The latter two of these proved not to contain any information on Wilson House. Two further potential sources were identified within the collection:
Boulton and Watt B&W 1 : Letter Book (Copies of Outgoing Letters) June 1775- Jan 1778
Boulton and Watt B&W 3 : Letter Book (Copies of Outgoing

Letters) Aug 1779- Dec 1781
Since all the correspondence from Wilkinson about the Wilson House engine dates from the second half of 1778, these volumes were not examined; unfortunately the intervening volume, which should have contained Watt's side of the correspondence over the engine, does not appear to survive.

The first mention of Wilson House occurs in a letter of 7th May 1776 (Box 20/2, 13), in which an engine is clearly under consideration. The main correspondence about Wilson House is found in three letters between August and November 1778, worth quoting in detail:

Box 20/2, 43

'Mr. James Watt, Engineer, at Redruth, Cornwall
Wilson House, 24th Augt 1778

Dear Sir

I have not long rec'd your Favor of the 17th past which has been defer'd answering a few Days, being desirous to give you some Acct of the Engine here.

We have had 3 tryalls since, Thomas said he was completely ready but have not succeeded yet to my Wishes in the working Gears - for I cannot have the Number of Strokes regulated, but must as we stand at present, work quick to tumble of[f] in the Loggerhead - & throw away full as much Air as we require for Use. - Consequently more Fuel must be burnt considerably than there is occasion for. Thos tells me that he cannot alter it so as to work fewer Strokes without hounding [?]. - However I have no doubt of getting the better of all this in a little time.

I have had Fire in the Furnace this Two Days & shall blow in 4 or 5 days - we got Steam with Peat exceedingly well & can readily create a Surplus. Have made up all the front Bars and I laid the bottom ones much closer by cutting of[f] the projections on one side. They now lay abt 7/8ths wide and admit sufficient air. When we get Iron I propose casting two Doors to fit close in the front to open occasionally in order to stir the fewell or close the Grate - at present it is wall'd up close. Getting sufficient Steam with Peat was what doubted most, that Suspicion is totally removed, for I observe we can work wth any Rubbish whatever. The making of Iron with this Sort of fewell will be the most Concern & of which I hope to be able to give some Acct in a fortnight or 3 Weeks. - If our regulating beam had been longer I fancy we shoud have done better with our Mechanism as to opening & shutting the Regulators - We are too near the Centre with our Plugg and this is the only difficulty that we seem to have upon our hands at present. We had a good deal of trouble with the perpendicular handing Valve at the hot Water Pump & was oblig'd to alter it before we coud get it to draw sufficient hot Water. Our Joints &c. are all very good - & with a Months practice I suspect to have a very competent Machine. If you can give Us any hint to regulate our Strokes so as to work slow, they may save time enough to be of Service in our Attempts to regulate [edge of page torn] I shall stay at least one Month [edge of page torn] & direction for Me to be left at the Dog & Duck in Kindale will find me most readily of any other address.

...I shall write again soon as I have made some Iron, meantime I remain very truly yours, John Wilkinson'

Box 20/2, 44

'Mr. James Watt, Engineer, Soho, near Birmingham Grange, Octr. 1st 1778

Dear Sir,

I am favor'd with yours of the 18th and observe wt you recommend at Wilson House. The working Gear for that Engine had been made long since, upon the Plan we work at Willey, but are now altering to 2 F Shafts having time to make such Alterations from some Repairs in the Furnace which I found necessary to make after we had blown about 4 days. I expect it will be about the middle of this Month before we get into Blast for good; & that I shall not get out of this part before Christmas.'

[the remainder of this letter deals with other mutual business]

Box 20/2, 45

Mr. James Watt, Engineer, Redruth, Cornwall (by Bristol)
Wilson House Nov. 15th 1778

Dear Sir,

Your Favor of the 7th I had last Night I never take much Credit in replying to your Letters whether Sick or well, in Humour or out of it. I make it a point to answer your Epistles the first Opportunity. - Considering what you have had under hand in Cornwall I dont wonder that both Body and Mind has been fully engag'd. I thank you for the Description of the Cataract tho' we have got two Fs that answer the Purposes of work very well.

We begun to blow again here on the 25th past with the Char Peat & Charcoal & make good strong Metal though it comes very dear. This day all that Coal is put on. Next tryale will be with the Peat Coal & raw Peat then Charcoal & raw Peat ringing all the Changes. I can think of procure a Metal strong as Bar Iron if possible. The Cost I shall not mind if I do but succeed in my pursuit of the strongest Cast Metal, which I flatter Myself I shall find out tho' as I observ'd before it will be <u>very</u> <u>dear</u>. Your Company for a Week here at this time woud be very pleasing. The different fluxes - & Cinders - together with the different Metal would I think be a high Treat to you - exclusive of the Engine which goes very pleasantly with any kind of rubbish Peat or even Peat Mule. Thomas has been proposing today to try Whins & Savin [?] from which you may infer that we can manage any Sort of light Fuel & that this Engine may pave the Way more readily for Erections where Coal is not to be had. But I must note that we have had a many retouches of our Grate & fire place, & have not yet done with Improvements in that part. However I am satisfy'd One of these Engines may be worked with Heath if no other Fuel offer'd. - A new Boyler might also be constructed to answer light fewell better - tho' this exceeds my expectations.

[The remainder of the letter deals with other matters. At the end however, he says]

...If any it a Month before I can leave this place & after L[ad]y Day I purpose to revisit it again. I have hue my troubles & Anxieties on these Experiments a certain Consequence in all new Undertakings where knowledge is to be gain'd by Experience. Do not take so much Credit to answer this Letter as you did the last & you will oblige him who is very sincerely yours

J. Wilkinson

A later list of engines made by Wilkinson at Bersham, to Watt's specification, identifies the Wilson House blowing engine as having a 27" cylinder (a very unusual size) (Tann 1981, 131; Ince 1992, 85).

Portfolio 695b contains two relevant drawings. The first is a set of detailed drawing of the nozzles, identified as for the Wilson House engine. The second (Fig 6) is an overall drawing of an unnamed 27" blowing engine; since the only other known 27" engine was a pumping engine for Cornwall, there is little doubt that this was the Wilson House engine. The engine is shown mounted within an 'all-indoor' engine house, which encloses the blowing cylinder as well as the steam cylinder, and has a central cross-wall on which the beam pivots; a condenser, water-pump and other accessories are mounted at basement level, and steam is supplied by a haystack boiler immediately outside the steam end of the engine house.

As noted above, later documents in the Boulton and Watt Papers have not been examined; correspondence with a fellow-researcher (Frank Dawson, pers. com.) indicates that they include references to purchases of lead and copper ore (from Parys Mountain, in which Wilkinson was a

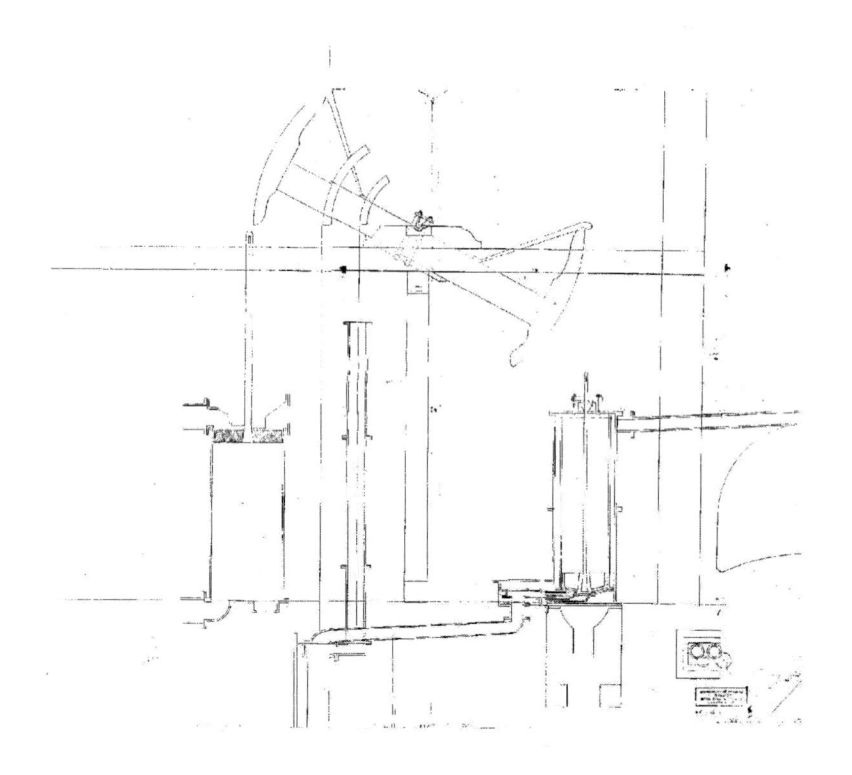

Fig 6. Blowing engine, almost certainly for Wilson House (Birmingham Public Library, Boulton and Watt Papers Portfolio 695b).

shareholder) for smelting at Wilson House in the early 1780s, presumably reflecting continuing and diversifying experiments.

Other sources

The other major iron industry source consulted was the

various lists of blast furnaces compiled by the industry in the later 18th century, used in their modern published forms. These comprise lists of charcoal furnaces in 1717, 1736, and 1750, and a list of charcoal furnaces closed between 1750 and 1788 (the latter in the Boulton and Watt records (Riden 1993)); lists of active furnaces (mainly coke) from 1790 onwards (Riden and Owen 1995), and a list of coke furnaces closed by 1788 (in the Boulton and Watt papers) (Riden 1992). None of these lists contain any mention of Wilson House; in view of their comprehensive nature, and Boulton and Watt's knowledge of Wilson House, this can be regarded as strong confirmation that Wilson House was regarded as a peat furnace which did not continue in blast using charcoal or coke, and had closed by 1790.

It should also be mentioned that Angerstein's diary contains no mention of Wilson House in its description of Furness (Berg and Berg (ed) 2001, 289-292). Angerstein was a Swedish ironmaster, who travelled extensively in England reporting on the iron industry and other industrial matters; he passed through Furness in autumn 1754, and his description includes lists of both furnaces and forges. Given his comprehensiveness and focus on the iron industry, it is unlikely that a working ironworks of any size would have escaped his attention.

The Field Evidence

A rapid record was made of the standing buildings (excluding obviously-modern agricultural sheds) and visible features, in gazetteer format; this is presented in summary form below, concentrating on Wilkinson-period elements. In addition to the formal record within the complex, the area to the north and east was rapidly examined for any evidence of a headrace and/or canal. Two possible candidates were observed, both surviving as wet or reed-filled hollows; one (reported by Davies-Shiel, and verified by observation) runs from the possible millpond north along the east edge of Wilson Hills, and the other lies along the east side of the former Stripes Lane, matching the possible water feature noted on the pre-1807 map. Both features are open to other interpretations, but it is possible that one or other marks a headrace, and/or the canal claimed by Stockdale. Davies-Shiel (pers. com.) also reports previous observations of haematite fines in the area west of building 22, and of 'copper slag' in the field southeast of buildings 19-21. The buildings divide into two complexes, referred to as the northern and southern farms (buildings 1-14 and 15-25 respectively).

Gazetteer

1 Vernacular barn, now much altered. Mid-19th century style (A Lowe pers. com.); the building is therefore interpreted as being of post-1847 date, on the site of earlier buildings.

2 External yard, forming entrance to farm from road. Metalled with stone cobbles and some brick, also exposed bedrock surfaces.

3 Boundary wall in vernacular style, with flat stone copings.

4 Small later-19th-century building, cut down from original size.

5 Single-story lean-to building of vernacular construction. Origin uncertain, due to mapping problems.

6 Northern farmhouse. Two-story, vernacular stone construction. N doorway protected by projecting canopy on

Fig 7. Ironworks area from NW 2002, possible charging ramp 17 in foreground building 1 to left and building 19 to

Fig 8. Building 24 from SE showing cast iron columns, and loading openings in rear wall.

kneelers. S doorway has porch supported by two cast iron columns or pipes. First mapped on one of pre-1807 plans; architectural style c 1800.

7 Extension to farmhouse, first clearly mapped in 1889. Mid C19th in architectural style.

8 Barn, of limestone rubble with segmental-arched doorways and windows. Roof of softwood king-post trusses, c 10m span. The architectural style suggests a date of c 1800-1820, but the style and quality are unusual for a vernacular barn. Roof probably a mid-C19th replacement.

9 Area to east of northern farm. Occupied by broad depression; north side formed by revetment wall (with building 10 built on its west end), with a stone platform along its base. Perhaps remains of millpond, or terminal basin of a canal.

10 Vernacular stone shed, lean-to roof, open north side held by one cast-iron pipe c 0.13m (5") diameter. Possibly shown on 1847 OS, first unambiguously mapped in 1889.

11 Milking parlour. Ground floor of vernacular stone, upper storey of brick. North gable wall has gauged brick voussoirs to flat-headed windows, and central segmental-headed upper window. Roof of waney oak collar and tie-beam trusses. The stone ground floor and the roof are of 18th-century vernacular style; the use of brick in a farm building is totally outside the Lake District tradition, but the style would appear compatible with late 18th-century Midlands brickwork.
Formed north end of L-shaped range, clearly visible on all mapping from pre-1807 onwards

12 Small building abutted to W side of 11. Vernacular

construction, slate roof.

13 Shippon. East and south walls of brick, over broader stone walls. West wall open, three bays held by cast iron columns (T-shaped in cross-section, with rounded end to 'downstroke'; asymmetric heads), plus fourth walled bay to south. 'Footprint' forms part of the L-shaped range on the pre-1807 map; the cast iron columns may therefore be *in situ* late 18th century structural ironwork.

14 Modern farm building (ruined), re-using 18th century pipes as pillars.

15 20th century dutch barn (ruined), using 18th century cast iron pipes as pillars. On a previous visit in 1984, some of these pipes were seen to bear the inscription 'Wilkinson 1784' (see also Davies-Shiel and Marshall 1971, 78).

16 Range of three 2-story cottages, now derelict. Style suggests 1830s-40s. On site of probable blowing house on pre-1807 maps.

17 Mound/knoll, with ramped access from north. The form of this feature is highly suitable for use as the charging platform of a blast furnace, which on this interpretation would be on the site of building 19.

18 Stone arch bridge across river Winster. Very well-built, stonework similar to building 8. Clearly shown on pre-1807 and later maps, but not on Yates' map of 1786. Below the bridge, the river flows against a vertical cut rock face on the north side; this, plus an unexplained line across the river on the pre-1807 map (a stop weir or lock?) may indicate canalisation of the river at this point.

19 Wide barn, of vernacular stone construction; masonry includes firebrick blocks, haematite and red sandstone fragments, copper-ore-stained blocks. Roof (partially collapsed) of high quality king-post construction with carpenters' marks; probably mid C19th. Structural complexities visible; parts of footprint match pre-1807 and 1807 maps, and may be mapped as roofless on (distorted) 1847 OS. Occupies site of probable furnace and casting house, and may incorporate fragments of the latter.

20 Ruinous 20th century pig-sties.

21 Catslide extension (original?) to north side of building 19.

22 Modern bungalow, on plinth of vernacular stone. Occupies summit of Jack Crag. Stone plinth probably stub of building shown on pre-1807 map; its shape and location would fit with interpretation as a charcoal, peat, or ore store. To the SW of building, a gateway is closed by an unusual cast-iron gate

23 Open-fronted building; 19th century, but much altered, perhaps cut down. Separate stone-built bay at north end, with low segmental arch to east. Open front held by three cast iron pipes (c 9" diameter, flange at top c 14"; 'WILKIN' cast in relief on one, with incised '7 3' below).

24 Brick open-fronted building, single-pitch roof. West wall has loading openings in upper part. E side open, held by two cast iron columns similar to those in 13; style of brickwork also similar to building 13. Footprint matches pre-1807 and 1807 maps, and form and location would fit with interpretation as a peat store for the blast furnace, with easy access to the interpreted boiler house and charging platform. The cast iron columns may therefore be *in situ* late 18th

century structural ironwork.

25 Southern farmhouse. Vernacular stone. Central block with flat-laid quoins on corners, mapped from pre-1807. East and west ends are extensions (edge-laid quoins, kneelers on eaves at corners), mapped from 1847. The location (commanding view of and access to the furnace area) suggests function as owner's or manager's house, the small size of central block suggesting the latter.

Discussion

There is at present no evidence for any ironworks on the site in the time of Isaac Wilkinson, although it apears that he did own or occupy the land from before 1750. It is unlikely that a blast furnace would have escaped the notice of Angerstein, or clear reference in the Furness iron industry documentation used by Fell and many later authors; while a small foundry or forge in Isaac Wilkinson's day remains possible, it is more likely that his occupation was entirely domestic and agricultural.

There is however clear evidence that John Wilkinson erected a steam-powered blast furnace in 1778, using the second blowing engine ever constructed (discounting the use of pumping engines to recycle water to primarily water-powered ironworks) (Ince 1992). This furnace was used for experiments in peat smelting, utilising various mixtures of raw peat, charred peat, and charcoal; the experiments would appear from Wilkinson's letters to have been technically successful, though not commercially viable. The works is perhaps best envisaged as a pilot plant, or even a 'hobby furnace'; the topography suggests that it may only have been c 4m high to charging level, less than the normal height of an 18th century charcoal furnace. The documents reported by

Dawson, supported by the copper-stained stonework observed on site, suggest that the furnace was then used for experiments in copper and lead smelting in the early 1780s. However there is no evidence for any continuing industrial use in Wilkinson's 1780s correspondence with Stockdale; although pipes and casting were stored there until at least 1791, the site appears as an agricultural part of the Castle Head estate.

The earliest known mapping of the site dates from shortly before 1807. This shows a T-shaped building complex at the south end; this looks nothing like normal Lake District farm plans of the period, but does bear comparison with late 18th century ironworks plans. It is therefore interpreted as the (disused) ironworks. By comparison with the Boulton and Watt drawing, and with known plans of other late 18th century ironworks, it is suggested that the semi-circular north end to this complex housed the haystack boiler, with the blowing engine house to its south (roughly on the site of building 16), and the furnace itself to the south again, with a casting house/foundry to its east, both on or near on the site of building 19; the field interpretation of area 17 as a charging platform, and the presence of metallurgical waste in the masonry of building 19, both support this reconstruction.

Assessment of the survival of features of the ironworks complex is complicated by problems with the 1st edition (1847) OS mapping. Assuming that this is distorted (perhaps due to cumulative mapping errors being 'lost' on the county boundary, which has occasionally been noted elsewhere in Cumbria (Alastair Oswald pers. com.)), it appears that much of the complex as mapped in 1807 was roofless in 1847, but was subsequently brought back into use; this interpretation is supported by the mid-19th stylistic dating of the windows of building 6, and the roofs of buildings 8 and 19, as opposed to the earlier dating of the masonry walls of the first two of these.

On this basis, building 16 occupies part of the site of the 1778 blowing house; the west wall, revetting the rising ground of the putative charging ramp, may prove to incorporate elements of the earlier building. The footprint of building 19 corresponds broadly to that of the pre-1807 building interpreted as the furnace and casting house/ foundry; in particular, a small eastwards extension from the SE corner, visible on both pre-1807 maps and the 1807 enclosure map, matches a similar feature on the 1889 OS map. While most of the standing building is of later date, it clearly includes re-used material from the ironworks buildings, and may incorporate some fabric of the original casting house.

Building 24 and the stone substructure of building 22 can also be identified, with more confidence, as dating from Wilkinson's time, since they are recognisable on every map from the pre-1807 onwards. Their location suggests storage buildings, building 22 perhaps being an ore store (on the basis of the haematite reported by Davies-Shiel), and building 24 perhaps a peat store (on the basis of its open-sided character, and loading openings in its west wall). The enigmatic structure to its south, recorded as part of building 23, might just possibly be the remains of a peat-charring kiln. It should be noted that the cast-iron columns holding the east side of building 24 are paralleled on site by those in building 13, and that the footprints of both buildings appear on the pre-1807 maps (whereas the map evidence is that none of the buildings held by the cast iron pipes can be traced back to the Wilkinson occupation). Buildings 24 and 13 may therefore retain Wilkinson's original late 18th century structural ironwork (whether cast on site or brought in from one of his other works), forming important early examples.

Bridge 18 can also be identified as a surviving part of Wilkinson's development of the site, though presumably relating to his agricultural rather than industrial activities.

The northern part of the site, as mapped in and before 1807, forms an enclosed compound clearly distinct from the southern buildings interpreted as the ironworks. This compound is interpreted as a late 18th century courtyard farm, presumably built by John Wilkinson, grafted onto an earlier vernacular layout (Wade Martins 2002, 41-67). As well as the iron columns of building 13 already noted, the use of brick in buildings 11 and 13 is unusual for the Lake District, and very unusual in a late 18th century agricultural context; this may relate to Stockdale's reference (1872, 211) to John Wilkinson making bricks from the clay below the peat on his mossland.

The cast iron pipes and columns on the site (especially those potentially in situ in 18th century contexts, but also the loose and re-used examples) are also of considerable technological importance, for their form, metallurgy, and foundry technology. In the light of the very short working life proposed for the furnace, and the 1784 dates formerly visible, it is suspected that the pipes were brought in by Wilkinson (probably from Bersham) rather than cast on site; this could be determined by archaeometallurgial examination to establish whether they are formed of coke-or peat-smelted iron, but their importance would remain high in either case. The columns are arguably of greater importance, being potentially *in situ* late 18th century structural ironwork. The cast iron gates, although portable rather than structural elements of the site, are also of interest.

Acknowledgements

My first debt must be to Paul Belford of Ironbridge archaeology, for undertaking the documentary work in Birmingham Reference Library. In addition, I am grateful to Mr and Mrs Dixon of Wilson House and Rebecca Gibson of John Coward Architects for commissioning the project and hospitality during fieldwork, to Andrew Lowe of Lake District National Park Authority for visiting the site with me and advising on the vernacular architecture and its dating, to John Hodgson and Eleanor Kingston of Lake District National Park Authority for help and advice, to Michael Davies-Shiel, George Demidowicz, and Dr Ron Fitzgerald for helpful information and advice on the industrial archaeology of the site, on the Boulton and Watt records, and on the cast iron beams respectively, to Frank Dawson for information on additional documentary sources, and to the staff of all the record repositories consulted or visited for their helpful service, especially Tim Proctor of Birmingham Reference Library for his guidance in finding the most relevant material within the Boulton and Watt collection.

Bibliography

Berg P and Berg T (trans), 2001. *R R Angerstein's Illustrated Travel Diary 1753-55* (London)
Cranstone D 1991. 'Isaac Wilkinson at Backbarrow', *Historical Metallurgy*, **25/2**, 87-92
Cranstone D 2002. *Wilson House, Lindale, Cumbria: Archaeological Desk-Based Assessment* (unpublished report to John Coward Architects and Lake District National Park Authority)
Davies-Shiel M and Marshall J 1971. *The Lake District at Work: past and present* (Newton Abbbot)
Ince L 1992. 'The Boulton and Watt Engine and the British Iron Industry', *Wilkinson Studies*, **II**, 81-90
Riden P 1992. 'Some unsuccessful blast furnaces of the early coke era', *Historical Metallurgy*, **26**, 36-44
Riden P 1993. *A Gazetteer of Charcoal-fired Blast Furnaces in Great Britain in use since 1660* (2nd edition) (Cardiff)
Riden P and Owen J G 1995. *British Blast Furnace Statistics 1790-1980*

(Cardiff)
Stockdale J 1872. *Annales Caermoelenses* (Ulverston)
Tann J 1981. *The Selected Papers of Boulton & Watt. Volume 1: the engine partnership 1775-1825* (London)
Wade Martins S 2002. *The English Model Farm* (Macclesfield)

HODBARROW MINE - INDUSTRY WITHIN AN INDUSTRY.

From Notes by the late Eric Holland.

The discovery of the huge Hodbarrow haematite deposit at Millom, with the extraction thereof overcoming serious obstacles, appeals strongly to the imagination and is certainly a tribute to the masters and men alike who played their individual parts in the adventure. Every mine has its story to tell: few however can be as dramatic at the Hodbarrow story.

The chronological history has been told elsewhere and what I want to do in this paper is to look at a rarely considered yet important factor - the relationship between the cost of pumping as shown by coal consumption and the output of ore. Weights of both coal and ore are given in Imperial Tons of 20cwt or 2240lbs. Figures are rounded to the nearest 5cwt.

Looking at the early years, say from around 1867, there was a ten-fold increase in coal consumption over the decade. Ore taken out over the same period certainly increased from about 133,000 tons to 192,000. It must have been heartening to the adventurers, but, it wasn't a ten-fold increase by any means. I had hoped that the coal consumption might, in some way, be indicative of the state of the mine, but as I examined the figures it became clear a far more complicated picture was emerging.

Output in those early years was coming from a number of small shafts, and possibly the deepening workings were encountering increasing amounts of water which had to lifted, possibly at the expense of ore. What appears to be the first major shaft sunk about this time was the 'Annie Lowther', equipped with steam winder and a beam engine pump. There was a jump in coal consumption when the shaft was commissioned in 1869, but no corresponding surge in output. About this time there were some nine steam boilers at various shafts, some quite small units.

The coal consumption did inexorably creep upwards though never, it seemed, linked to production. In due course trade downturns, the odd strike, but especially the serious inrushes of sand, water and clay from the overlying cover were to have their effects upon ore production, though not to a great extent on coal consumption.

The coal books do provide information on what was working at any time, and how much particular items of plant were burning. Practically all of the coal was used for steam production. In 1897 some 2,572 tons of coal were used, and ore output for that year was about 472,000 tons. During 1903 something like 2,313 tons of coal were consumed against 445,000 tons of ore raised. There did seem to be a correlation between output and coal usage at this time.

At this time most of the early shafts had been superseded by other deeper and better equipped shafts. All were steam powered. Extensions to the ore-body were to be mined from No. 1 (William); No. 5 (Arnold); No. 6 (Rock Shaft); and in due course No. 7 which was actually put down contiguous to No. 6; and also the No. 8 Shaft. Lowther Pit was sunk quite close to the old Annie Lowther Shaft which was probably struggling with the increasing output. Nos. 5 & 8 as well as Annie Lowther and the new Lowther were equipped with large beam-engine pumps. Later, in 1910, No.10 Shaft was sunk close to No. 8 and was fitted with a large beam engine pump taking its steam from No 8's boiler plant. These pumps were capable of lifting up to 50% mix of sand and pebbles with the water.

The great beds of ore were worked by the time-honoured 'Top-Slice Caving' method which was responsible for a great area of surface subsidence known as The Hollow. This ever deepening depression was a natural gathering place for

Fig. 1. No 10 shaft (nearest camera) and No 8 shaft prior to demolition.

surface water and three somewhat fuel-greedy steam pumps were installed here for essential water control. In 1903 these pumps took 138 tons. It was an unavoidable cost. Coal provision was also made for key staff houses, the Office, and the Captains' Dry. This amounted to 140 tons.

Fuel was also demanded by the locomotives which not only delivered materials about the mine (including coal and timber), but also handled the ore production to the Millom ironworks, the quay for shipping, and the main railway sidings.

Even in these early years of the twentieth century the mine had expanded over an area of about three-quarters of a square mile. The surface distance from No. 1 Shaft to No. 8 was over half a mile. Another shaft No. 11 (Moorbank) which came on stream in August 1931 was distant from No. 8 by about three quarters of a mile. All of the shafts were interconnected by the underground workings. However, Moorbank Shaft was electrically powered from the start. Nevertheless coal was consumed by the locomotives taking materials to the shaft, and bringing away the ore. Indeed, the more I looked at the scene of these busy steam locos backwards and forwarding on the network of rails the more I felt I was seeing an 'industry within an industry'.

The 1920s and 1930s were years of industrial depression. For Hodbarrow the worst trading years were 1921 to 1925; indeed in 1921 orders were so much reduced that temporary closures were followed by men being laid off. At this time No. 1 Shaft was mainly in use for men and materials but in 1921 took only 6¾ tons for its boiler. No. 6 Shaft had 13 deliveries totalling 256½ tons during January of that year; 82¾ tons in February, and a delivery of 44¼ tons in March. Then after a drop of 18½ tons in July no more was taken to its hopper until the year end. The Hollow's pumps could not be stopped and in the same year had 637¼ tons. Nos. 8 & 10 shafts could not be stopped either and took no less than 1,645 tons in that year. During September Lowther Pit was brought back into use for a short while, possibly to assist with pumping. For 1921 3,320 tons of coal were used all-in-all, whilst ore output plummeted to a low of 43,928 tons. During one shift in that year No. 8 Shaft raised seven bogies of ore containing three and a half tons

Fig. 2.The Lowther shaft taken from the old Annie Lowther Shaft.

In order to reduce the consumption of coal, together with some concerns over the state of some of the old machinery, a decision was made to partially electrify the works. This was finished during 1926. New and more efficient boilers were installed, which as well as supplying steam for No. 6 winder also supplied a 500kw steam turbo-generator. No. 5 Shaft winder was electrified, though its beam pump was left with steam. No.7, alongside No. 6, was converted to electric drive, along with No. 1 which was now acting as a furnace-assisted up-cast shaft as well as handling men and materials. Compressed air was supplied (from No. 6 power station) by a

Bellis & Morcom steam unit capable of providing 1,000 cubic feet per minute. A smaller steam-powered generator was installed at the No. 8 Shaft (taking steam from its boiler house) to provide emergency power for pumps in the lower levels of the mine which in turn fed water to the beam pumps' sumps. This generator was in use at weekends for lighting when the main turbine was stopped. The coal consumed during 1923 is recorded as 1,923 tons against an ore yield of 137,558 tons.

The mine had always been troubled by influxes of water, sand and clay from the continually subsiding strata above. Working places, ore-passes. ladder-ways, and even main haulageways might be filled with material. It was an intolerable burden on finances.

A particularly bad inrush took place in April of 1933. At this time No. 6 (Rock Shaft), and No. 8 were the main producers. No. 10 was on stand-by and No. 5 was mainly a pumping shaft. During the week ending 15th April No. 6 sent up 1,161 bogies of ore (593¾ tons) together with 179 bogies of stone which was fairly typical. In the same week No. 8 raised only 32 bogies of ore (16 tons) but also lifted 561 bogies containing 7cwt of sand. No. 10 Pit was brought into service to assist in the emergency and raised 383 bogies of sand. The following week saw No. 8 bring up only four bogies of ore, but 649 of sand, while the adjacent No. 10 Shaft lifted 400 sand bogies. By now No. 6 Shaft, although raising ore, began to be hindered by the sand. Only 31 bogies of sand were raised to start with, but there were 187 bogies of the inevitable stone.

Worse was to follow. For the week ending April 29 No. 8 raised no ore, just 1,517 bogies of sand, whilst No. 10 drew 1,352. No. 6 Shaft remained affected until early August by which time it had drawn 2,073 bogies of sand, 730 of stone, together with 29,347 tons of ore.

But for No. 8 Shaft the position was far more serious. Week after week the cages had brought to surface up to 3,730 bogies of the wet clayey sand, and not until September 1934 did the problem appear to have been mastered. No. 10 Shaft, which had been in action for 13 weeks, brought to surface 21,493 bogies of sand, whilst No. 8 raised 72,531. In all the workmen had had to clear 96,097 bogies. It was not just their wages which had to be covered. Raising this stuff cost money in the form of steam, which was created by coal. There was the inevitable loss of output, not to mention the considerable wear and tear on machines and equipment.

This clearing up period did, in fact, see a disastrous slump in production. Even including the steadily increasing production from No. 11 Shaft, the sum total never exceeded 100,000 tons in any year. The coal issued is recorded at 425¾ tons for 1933 and 782¼ tons for 1934. Taking all into account, these are surprisingly low figures. The ore drawn in 1933 and 1934 was 56,908 and 76,584 tons respectively.

In an attempt to stem the inflow of water freezing had been resorted to with apparent success, at least until early in 1934 when sea-water once again poured in. Ore output had increased even though much was filled into hoppers, or tipped on the 'bank' as stock. The new inrush must have been viewed with intense dismay amongst masters and men as the work of clearing the last influx was largely undone. Once again the 70 Fathom Level workings, and main haulageways were flooded and sand filled. Market conditions being as they were, it was decided to abandon the workings reached from No. 8 Shaft, lying between the Old Sea Wall and the Outer Barrier and these remained closed until World

War II brought an increased demand for ore.

Fig. 3.The Old Sea Wall is seen collapsed into the Hollow.

83,920 tons of ore were raised during the year 1935, the output being sustained by production from Moorbank Mine and the No. 1 Shaft area. Also Red Hills ore was raised at No. 6 Shaft; while ore from No. 5 district was hauled to No. 8 Shaft. Leavings in the Old Mine workings were examined and what could be won was brought out via No. 8 Shaft. Coal consumption for the year came to 818 tons with the No. 6 boilers (which powered the steam generator, and compressor, and the No.6 steam winder) receiving the lion's share of 682 tons. No. 8 boiler house had only 17 tons; probably just enough, with scrap wood, to effect control of the mine water. This was almost certainly kept down by the No. 10 Shaft cages which were equipped with tanks. The low coal tonnage suggests that the beam pumps could not have been operating. Water in the 70 Fathoms Level was allowed to rise to the horizon of the 60 Fathom Level where it was held by electric pumps feeding the sumps of the beam pumps. The bucket lifts had been disconnected.

Fig. 4. The Old Sea wall is seen subsided into the Hollow. In the far distance is the Outer Barrier. The pumps have been stopped and the water is beginning to rise.

In this manner the mine was kept afloat, in more than one sense, and in 1940 88,591 tons of ore were raised of which 30,094 came up No. 11 (Moorbank Mine). Coal for this period amounted to 857 tons.

Ten years on the same shafts delivered to surface 105,079 bogies representing 53,286½ tons. The coal delivered on site amounted to no less than 5,727 tons. No.5 boilers took 1,755 tons; No. 8 both winding and pumping heartily with the beam engines in operation, took 3,096 tons. The locomotives had 562, the blacksmiths 8½. The Office, Captains' Dry, and the houses, were allocated 139 tons. Just less than 200 tons was even put into stock.

The costs of running the steam pumping at Nos. 8 and 10 Shafts were not unnoticed by management. Nor was the inrush in the No. 1 Shaft workings in October 1955, which caused great disruption, and damage to electrical equipment, and was not brought under control until well into 1956. A major disaster occurred during 1958 when timbering in the stand-bye No. 7 Shaft broke away and crashed through into the contiguous No. 6. This effectively prevented further exploitation of the Red Hill deposit, as well as stopping production in the No. 1 Shaft district. It left No. 8 and No.11 Shafts to support the running costs of the property.

The amount of ore from No.8 Shaft was reducing fast and had been for some time. Finally Shafts 8 and 10 were abandoned for ore raising in October 1958. Since September

Fig. 5 'Snipey', the Neilson Crane Engine delivers wood to No 11 shaft.

1st only 374 bogies of ore (181½ tons) of ore had been wound, along with 150 bogies of sand and 186 of rock. Hodbarrow now had only one shaft to sustain it, No. 11 (Moorbank).

Pumping could not cease at Shafts 8 and 10 however, for uncontrolled flooding could be expected to overwhelm Moorbank's pumping capability in time despite its distance away. During 1960 some 761¾ tons of coal were used, with the output from No. 11 coming to 31,334 tons in that year. Submersible electric pumps were installed in the No.10 shaft, which brought the coal consumption down to 360 tons in total for 1961.

Fig. 6 Nos 8 and 10 shafts adjacent to the Old sea Wall. The old lighthouse can be seen in the background.

The end of Moorbank Mine was now in sight. In 1967 the mine yielded 28,439 tons of ore averaging 568 tons per week. Coal used came to 210 tons.

The final year, 1968, saw the mine shut down. The last week

of production was that ending 23rd March. 103 men lost their jobs. During the last twelve weeks the miners had sent up 7,198 tons of ore, an average of 600 tons per week. Coal delivered was one wagon (No. 420883 from Whitehaven) which brought a meagre 18 tons, of which 10 tons went to the houses and office, and the remainder to the locomotives still in use. These were a 1930 Peckett, a Hunslet of 1882; and the wonderful 1890 Neilson crane engine, 'Snipey'.

Hodbarrow Mine was located virtually on the sea shore, and wet conditions must have been expected from the outset. They certainly led to enormous expense in the pumping infrastructure and the tidal barriers. Coal was consumed in great quantities prior to partial electrification, but even after the installation of the turbo-generating set steam was still required to power the same; albeit raised in more efficient boiler plant. The calamitous inrushes below surface (which could nudge the whole enterprise into unprofitability for a while) meant that little correlation could be found between coal consumption and ore production. Steam was still required for pumping, and winding sand clay & stone, regardless of the actual ore tonnage raised. The "Hollow" is filled with water, but plenty remains on site to make this a most interesting visit for the industrial archaeologist.

MILLOM - THE END GAME

By Dr. David Robson Davis

This paper is concerned with the final developments at the Millom Hematite Ore and Iron Co. Ltd. and how it came to develop Spray Steelmaking.

The background to this is that in the early 1960s the Millom company was a subsidiary of the Cranleigh Group and as such was well backed financially. Ore came from Hodbarrow, less than a mile away, and while these ores were almost exhausted the firm also owned Florence Mine some 20 miles north. Foreign ores imported through nearby Barrow Docks were also an important part of the blend. The firm owned a coke-making plant in Durham and the local Goldmire limestone quarry.

The plant had been well maintained and continuously modernised, with a new blast furnace in 1961. As a result it could produce first class merchant pig iron with extremely close control of specifications. It was also noted for its high quality ingot moulds and other heavy castings which it sold to the steel industry.

In 1964 when the writer took on commitment to Millom the future looked bleak for the steel industry with declining demand for iron and steel affecting European and World producers. Within the UK there was not only an outcry about unfair competition from overseas but the Private Sector was critical of the political situation, in which it had to compete with a subsidised Public Sector.

This paper concentrates on the particular challenges

and also on how these challenges were approached.

The merchant pig iron dominated the business and there appeared to be no future for the company unless we could continue exploiting our substantial blast furnace capacity. Up to this time this had meant selling iron to a) the cold-metal acid open-hearth steelmakers, mainly operating in the Sheffield area and b) to the many local iron foundries scattered throughout Britain. Unfortunately, the stark truth was that both these markets were shrinking and likely to continue to do so.

Low sulphur low phosphorus hematite iron, a Millom speciality, was the ideal feed for acid steelmaking. Sadly, acid open-hearth steelmaking, long established for high quality applications, had been gradually losing ground to the basic electric process which operated on a scrap steel feed and not on pig iron. The dramatic decline in acid open-hearth is seen in Fig. 1.

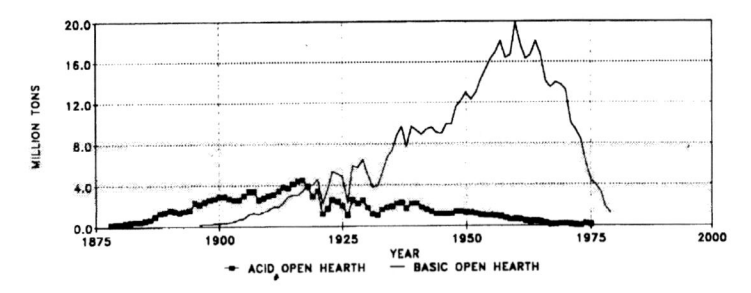

Fig. 1 UK steel production by acid and basic open hearth processes.

In the other market, while pig iron for ironfoundry demand was reasonably steady up to the middle 1960s, developments in train were not encouraging and Figs. 2 and 3 show how

UK outlets for foundry iron were destined to decline rapidly in the 1970s. The causes were threefold. i) A general fall in the UK usage of iron castings. Plastics were ousting iron in several applications, such as pipes. ii) The development of Ductile iron, a brand of iron based on a patented process using steel scrap instead of pig iron. iii) The advent of continuous casting in steelmaking was rendering the use of ingot moulds obsolescent. Ingot mould manufacture required a hematite pig iron feedstock and Millom would be severely affected by this loss of market. Already Millom's own foundry was feeling the effect of the decline in demand for these moulds.

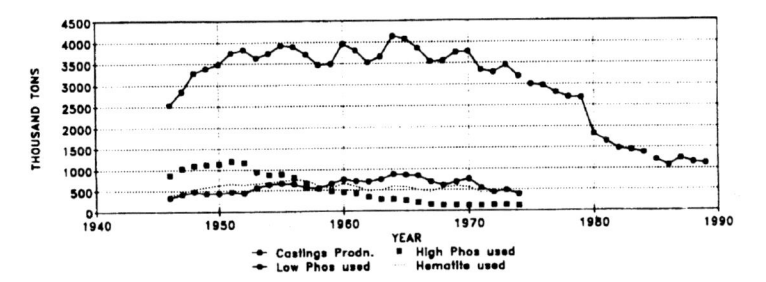

Fig. 2. UK production iron castings by product group.

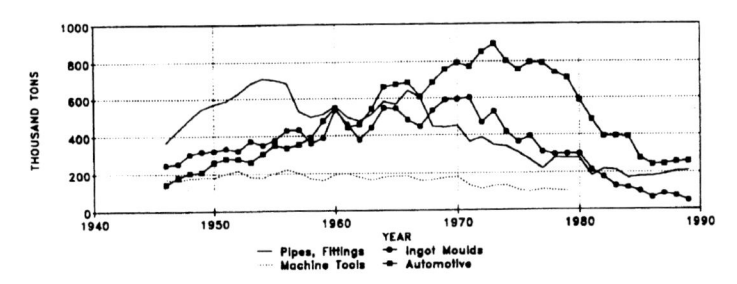

Fig. 3. UK castings production and iron consumption by pig iron type.

The only way to exploit Millom's substantial ironmaking capacity in the future was to develop a steelmaking business. Well-founded conventional wisdom pointed to economic new plants based on liquid iron feed, exploiting the latest oxygen converters and needing a large-scale production of upwards of a million tons per year. Such a proposition was never considered as a serious possibility at Millom which was limited by its blast furnace capacity to around 350,000 tons. It was therefore essential to find an innovative steelmaking process viable at a relatively low tonnage using existing ironmaking capacity. Our aim was to establish a modest profitability at an output of 150,000 tons of steel billets in Phase 1, with the prospect of a high return on doubling this output in Phase 2.

In pursuing a process with low capital cost the approach was to eliminate the usual concept of a separate steelworks with all its ancillary equipment and buildings, and instead to make steel with a 'bolt-on' apparatus for treating liquid iron as it left the blast furnace.

At this stage Millom consulted The British Iron & Steel Research Association (BISRA) in Sheffield. It emerged that following earlier experiments at RTB Redbourn, aimed at developing an effective desiliconising process, BISRA had built a laboratory plant to explore the conditions for the removal of silicon, carbon, sulphur amd phosphorus from remelted pig iron, using a spray technique. It was obvious that collaboration with Millom would offer mutual benefits and no time was lost in getting samples of Millom iron to Sheffield for melting and spraying in the BISRA chamber. After a period of experimentation correct conditions for conversion to a low-carbon iron were established, and Millom decided to design and install a substantial works-scale pilot plant. This would embody the principle of making steel at the blast furnace, using the know-how, advice and help of BISRA. The term Millspray was applied exclusively to the Millom system of linking BISRA's spray process to the blast furnace runner and in turn integrating with a continuous casting. Millspray Ltd. was set up as a consulting company wholly owned by the Millom concern. A detailed account of the process was published in the *Journal of the Iron & Steel Institute* (see below). Low-carbon, medium-carbon and high-carbon steels were all successfully produced.

Figures (4) and (5) show the plant during a steelmaking run. The stopper rod in the centre of Fig. (5) controlled the discharge of iron from the furnace runner. The ladle was lined with magnesite bricks. Surplus iron flowed into an iron ladle for pig casting. The spray developed as oxygen jets and a lime curtain struck the treated iron just below the ring in the centre of the water-cooled magnesite roof. There was a gap between the upper chamber and the ladle to allow air entrainment, and fume was extracted to a discharge chimney via a side flue. Scrap was placed in the ladle beforehand but small additions could be made via the chute. The steel collected in the ladle, which could hold 10 tons, and formed the lower half of the chamber. When it was full the slag ran over into the slag pot and the ladle was drawn away. Steel was made at 35 tons per hour. To the right of Fig. (4) is the hopper from which lime was discharged into the flux ring at the point of oxygen injection.

Inevitably there were many problems to be overcome but the rate of progress in solving them justified the company's decision to design a commercial scale Millspray system linking ironmaking, steelmaking and continuous casting.

Fig. 4. Withdrawn ladle of steel (in effect the lower part of the spray chamber) ready for alloy addition.

Fig. 5.Blast furnace discharging iron via tundish stopper (centre of picture) into spray chamber.

Many re-rolling companies gave assurances of interest in the proposed product. Especially attractive to them was the potential availability of low-cost, low-residual, carbon steel billets for rolling into rods and wire.

Proceeding from pilot plant scale to commercial scale, involving as it would substantial investment, required the company to seek approval from the iron & Steel Board (ISB) under the 1953 Iron and Steel Act. This was done in September 1966. Although the ISB had publicly praised the success of the Millom pilot development, three months of indecision eventually elicited a statement of reluctance to give support to the project and turning down the application or, more evasively, deferring a decision. Months of futile appeal left the prospect of progress increasingly hopeless and work on the pilot plant, work that involved substantial expense, had to be suspended.

After a further three months prevarication, months critical to Millom's survival, the ISB facing the charge that it was in breach of its statutory duties, produced a statement that Millom's plan was undesirable but admitting that Phase 1 development was on a scale debarring the ISB from refusing consent under the terms of the Act.

Thus, while ultimately accepting the illegality of its blocking efforts the ISB had, through its delaying tactics, thwarted Millom's ambitions and delivered the kick that would undermine fatally the company's prospects and its standing in the financial markets.

Thus concluded Millom's 'End Game'. All operations ceased in August 1968.

REFERENCES
Davies, D.R.G. Steelmakers of Millom. Journal Historical Metallurgy Society, Vol 29, No 1. 1995
Davies, D.R.G; Rhydderch, M.J; & Shaw, L.J. Journal of the Iron & Steel Institute, JISI 205, 1967.

BACKBARROW FURNACE AND ITS HISTORY FROM 1868-1967.

By Mike Davies-Shiel

Position alongside a railway-line is Everything.

Backbarrow Furnace was put up for sale in 1818. By sheer luck it was bought by the co-owners of Newland Furnace, Harrison & Ainslie, to act as its 'twin' furnace. The intention was at the time quite clear, that Backbarrow Furnace would always be in blast for any time that Newland Furnace had to be out of blast for re-lining, repairs, and improvements.

The chosen route of the Furness Railway extension to Lancaster in 1857 by-passed Newland, by one mile so that all goods inwards and cast iron out had to be loaded and carried in carts to and from the line. When the very profitable tourist rail link was built to Lakeside at the foot of Windermere in 1868, it passed immediately behind Backbarrow's ore, fuel, flux and scrap store houses. Harrison Ainslie & Co. at once initiated sidings and improved and enlarged all the store housings.

However, before the new rail link past Backbarrow was made, Newland already had plans afoot to enlarge their own furnace from 25 tons maximum capacity to 30 tons, and to convert to hot blast in the manner of the times. While's manuscript gives the maximum weekly casts at Newland of 27ton -10cwt in 1872. As a result Newland would be out of production for two to three years. Bonawe Furnace (also owned by the firm) in Scotland had closed in

1866, so Backbarrow and a newly built charcoal furnace at Warsash in Hampshire would continue the Newland 'makes' for their large list of customers. Mr. Dickinson, their skilled furnace manager, went to Warsash . By 1873 Newland was in hot blast, with a flue built into the stack to take exhaust gases down to an air-heating oven or stove. Two cupolas had been built to continue cold blast makes for fastidious customers. In the next few years, as Newland learnt anew how to make good iron with a hot-blast Warsash was slowly wound down, closing finally in 1877.

The above data is needed because Backbarrow Furnace perforce copied Newland in 1888 when she too went hot blast. There were immediate savings in fuel and a 7% increase in yield of iron from the same ore. (Like ships and aircraft, furnaces were always Women - producers giving birth, but never Ladies, being always too 'Awkward', 'Perverse', 'Stubborn' and 'Stupid' or, unprintably, worse! At best, in the jokey speech of the furnace gang, she was 'alright.) Her job, of course, was in early years until the start of World War I in 1914 to produce a range of pig irons across ten approximate qualities, each with six items of non-ferrous content, as expected by forge and foundrymen everywhere in the western world.

The non-ferrous additives and the proportions used determined the differing forge and foundry qualities. The additives used were graphitic carbon, combined carbon, silica, sulphur, phosphorus and manganese. In the pre-1919 years the ten iron qualities sold went largely by the fresh-broken colour of pigs. These were: No. 1 Grey (Soft); No. 2; No. 3 Grey (Hard); Very Soft Mottled; Low Mottled; Hard Mottled; High Hard Mottled; Soft White; Speckled White and White (so hard that it was held to unmachinable prior to the cutting tool improvements of WWII). In the A5 size notebooks and other places they were written in initialese as G1, G2, G3, VSM, LM, HM, HHM, SW, Spk, and W. It took some time to find out their meaning and significance. Almost nothing in the documents was ever explained.

By 1925 the larger customers were already demanding their pigs by formulae, but new-comers and small firms still clung to the ten old names in initialese until the 1950s. They also asked for the coldblast pigs of 'Lorn', 'Leven', 'Grazebrook' and 'Backbarrow Refined', until the 1930s. Customers ranged from tiny forges to world-renowned firms, including 200-300 from Italy and Germany to Pennsylvania in the U.S.A., wherever in fact there were concentrations of heavy industry. Firms such as Ford, Fiat, Chrysler, Daimler and Austin; also Aveling & Porter, Robey, Ruston & Hornsby, Baldwins, Davy United Rolls, J. Guest, and Stuart & Lloyds of South Wales, Singer Sewing Machines, Westinghouse Brake & Signal, Armstrong Whitworth, Vickers & Maxim, and Woolwich Arsenal show the huge range of industries supplied. Backbarrow lost two of her best "bread-and-butter" firms, Fiat and Ford, when they set up huge new works after WWII and demanded outputs that the tiny furnace just could not meet. 500tons per month was too small!

There are hundreds of analyses jotted down by the Backbarrow chemists, of every sort of material that came into their hands, none of which threw any light on how such a scruffy little rough stone furnace could make such accurate formulae to a tolerance of less than four thousands of 1%, from 1919 to the 1967 closure.

So at last I had to contact my friend Jack Lancaster (the acknowledged steel expert who lives in Cumbria), and put to him my thinking that they must have put every cast into specific stacks of differing contents into the stockyard, having on each the cast number burnt into a strip of wood, which tallied with the formula discovered by the analyst. That is, they did not make to order but what was made went into Contents Piles in the yard. And when a Customer asked for a particular formula he got the pile or piles, each the capacity of the extant ladle, that had that formula. Jack, patient man, said to me that I had answered my own question. So that was how it was done! Whew! what a relief! So, the only "Art and Mystery" was when to tap!

Backbarrow's Stockyard could hold well over 5,000 tons of pigs, whereas Newland could only hold about 2,500 Tons, which was not enough to keep customers satisfied if a major upset occurred. By 1886 the Company must have begun to rationalise plans and decided to close down Newland, with its small two-tuyere hearth. With cheap Spanish ores coming on the market, Newland's hematite iron mines were losing customers, and trans-shipment costs at Newland were increasing rapidly. But as we have seen, before doing so Backbarrow had to go hot blast too, so as to maintain stocks of the 'makes' that customers wanted. In 1870, before going hot blast themselves in 1873, the Newland company had put in a larger furnace at Backbarrow, together with a larger and more flamboyant lintel!

Before the Backbarrow site got its Hot Blast furnace a bell was fitted, in 1886, and an identical flue on the stack's casting side, leading to a hot-air stove of drystone walling, which I could identify from similar structures attached to early captioned furnace photos elsewhere. I had been lucky to obtain the text of a lecture of 1924 by Professor Henry Louis of Durham to the Sheffield Society of Engineers & Metallurgists on iron-making which included a shot of Backbarrow Furnace but only with the unhelpful title 'Fig. 6'. I can date it to 1888, for the fairly new railway track in

Fig. 1. Hot air charcoal blast furnace at Backbarrow, c. 1888. Note drystone-walled single stove; water-lift on uphill side of stack; and large sows stacked on the stockyard.

the background and a new engine house in left foreground are quite clear. Professor Louis was called in by the newly-formed Backbarrow Charcoal Iron Co. of 1905. He helped with the technicalities of installing 2 redbrick stoves by 1908 and a better bell. Without much expertise, and with hot stoves not well made, there were many times when furnacemen complained of 'only warm' or 'cold again' and Backbarrow sales went down badly. Note also the tall 1855 Waterlift attached to the west face of the stack, with its balancer tank built on the hillside above the site of the railway line. The system permitted a handcart containing 4cwt of ore/fuel plus one man to be lifted effortlessly to the stack top. The stepped wall sheltered the men from the elements and a projecting buttress containing the hot gas flue went down and out to the top of the dry-stone stove. [The 1888 stack ref. is BDB/2/9/1]

The lower stone stack visible today was constructed in 1770, about 60m. south of the original 1711 stack but using fresh, unburnt stone from an old fulling mill across the river Leven. The old stack lived a few years longer until around 1773 whilst John (Iron mad) Wilkinson did peat experiments with briquettes and charcoal, which proved effective. (Indeed, Backbarrow was to use peats for several campaigns until the 1870's to eke out charcoal shortages, since by then the bobbin industry took much of the coppice harvest grown across Cumbria - my research.) The 1770 stone stack, rebuilt to 32ft high, survived until 1888, when the top 10ft were taken off and replaced with redbrick outer walls. The hot gas flue was reconstructed vertically into the new redbrick casting-arch wall, just north of centre, as shown on a 1912 company photo. The present stack still retains a vertical slot built into the same face, but it is now to be found slightly south of centre of that wall. There is no obvious reason for its retention. There was no rebuilding done above bosh level in

1962 (my observations on site), so the stack as seen in 2003 was rebuilt in the 1927 alterations when the hot blast charcoal furnace changed to coke fuel. The new waterlift tower to a bridge across the new road of 1921 (built by the local County Council) was constructed in 1922 and was retained until closure in 1967.

Other ancillary buildings included a second charcoal store which was used for steel-turnings from Birmingham after 1921; also there was more space for limestone once coke fuel was used from 1927, the extra limestone taking the place of 'lithomarge'. This was a type of kaolin from Ulster, used as a flux and resulting in highly-coloured glassy slags which fooled many 18th century experts and the Millom Furnace Co. too! Since an Ulsterman originally built the furnace, he may well have introduced its use here.

The Pug Mill, so-called for its production of the pugged clay and ganister spear used to plug the furnace tap-holes at the end of casts has, at its east side alongside the river what was part of Machell's forge of 1685. In 1866, it became the housing for the first turbine, 8½ hp on a 10ft head; followed in 1869 by a 40 hp unit on 14½ft head. Although reliable the turbines did not replace the waterwheel until c.1888, by which time there was also a stand-by steam engine for times of drought and which was still working in 1943. The western part of the Pug Mill contained a large joinery unit for making the timber casts and moulds for urban waterpipes and other large items, these were trundled on rails around to the foundry shed east of the furnace stack. Above the moulding shed was a large blacksmith's shop with 2 small forges, bellows, anvils, swages etc., also a small store holding the metal 'Make-named' pig-stamps. Over the years from 1870 several other forges, an anchor smithy, and foundries were erected and, in due time, demolished.

One other aspect of conversion to hot blast was the immediate need to construct cupolas. These were vertical tubular hearths, firebrick lined, which could produce yields per day of up to 120 tons, making cold blast iron as still demanded by foundries until the 1950s. From 1921, the While family directors researched one sure way to higher profitability. This was the manufacture of Ingot Moulds. Whilst the largest such items were circa 25 tons or more in weight, there were many foundries across the western world that made smaller items such as cast-iron wall-boxes for electrical fuses, small aluminium cases, etc., for which only a light-weight casting was needed. They set up a South Cupola with its own 'runway' for moulds from a ½ ton to 5 tons. Instead of a few shillings profit on a pig of iron from the furnace, the mark-up rose to some 300-400%. If the foundry-customer had a large order then over time many replacements would be needed. From 1922 to 1965 Backbarrow made steady profits from this one outlet. I was not permitted to see this unit at work, since most goods were patented and products guarded against any form of industrial spying, no matter how innocuous!

However, statistical outputs for the South Cupola could be analysed and I noted the term 'ladle', in the cupola's day's notebooks, was always set against casts of 2 tons to 3½ tons which fitted the original machinery orders when the ingot-mould plant was being set up. By the 1950s, the S cupola was replaced by one producing up to 5 ton casts and thus made its own iron for moulds, releasing the furnace to make bulk customers' orders for foundries in the eastern U.S.A. The Americans insisted upon pigs for all their foundries, containing exactly 1% of Silica, when all Cumbrian hematite ores had only 0.4% Silica in them. Customers could be fooled though, for demands for cold blast pigs came from the

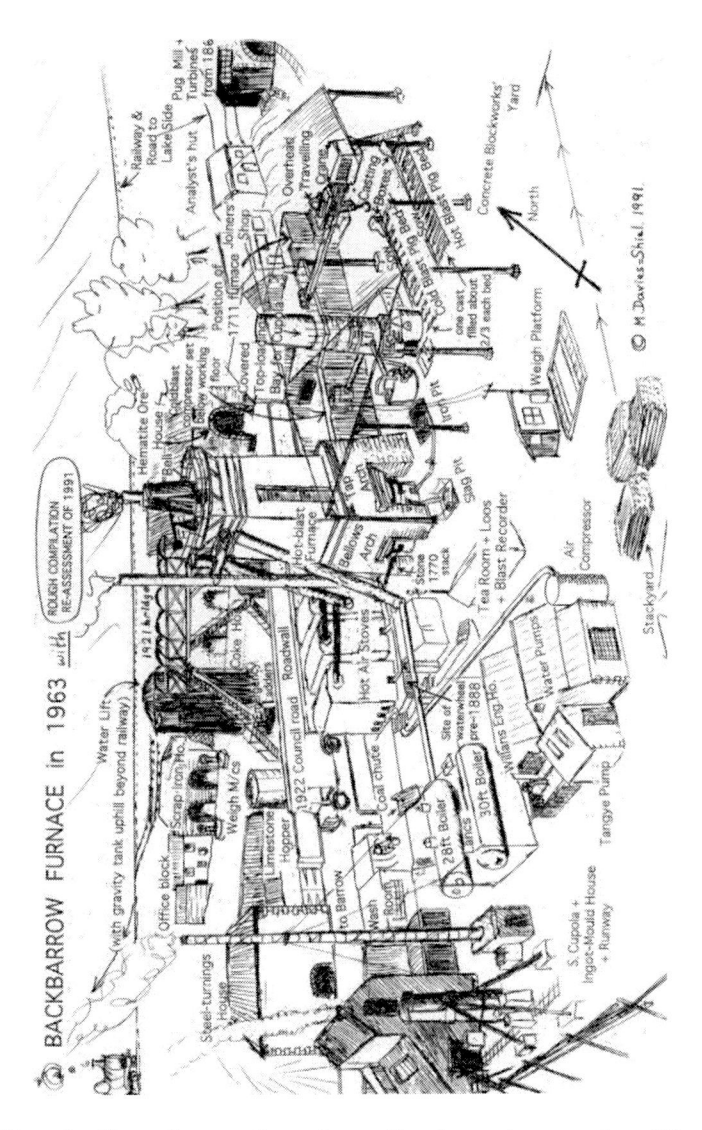

Fig. 2. Functions of each unit given to me by Mr. D.A.While, owner, in 1991. Length of view from S.Cupola to L corner of Pugmill, c.312ft/97 metres

cupolas usually and not the furnace that had hitherto made them. No-one ever complained.

Unfortunately for the record or 'posterity', I took no photos either of the North Cupola at work. It finished completely two weeks before permission was given to photograph the furnace in action. However Mr. Baines, the Foreman, did say that in spite of using motorised trolleys the cupola was so thirsty that ten men were kept in a high sweat all day feeding the brute. It gobbled well over 200 tons of raw material to make 120 tons of iron per day. The trolleys were kept in the 'Roaster House' at the base of the furnace stack each night. In earlier years, yellow-hot pigs were placed on crushed hematite ore there to 'improve' it. Certainly, a toughness was thereby imparted to new pigs.

Over the years from 1868 to its closure Backbarrow's foundrymen's techniques changed with ever new demands from industry. The furnace team spent much time in the hungry '30s making small and recorded changes to the content of each charge smelted, until by 1931 they had a regularly large yield of the makes most needed by their customers. First-time customers got good samples of the old labelling of quality makes. Backbarrow had also specialised in producing chills for prestigious firms that wanted extremely hard-wearing surfaces such as in rock-crusher jaws, small pieces of White Iron being set into the sand-lining of pig beds with square cross-sections. Surfaces melded into a steel-like quality for the whole pig. Chills were of high commodity value, like ingot-moulds.

The only real 'mystery' was knowing when to tap the furnace. 'Front-side' furnacemen watched the surface of the iron through spyholes or 'Peepes', set through each tuyere. They were looking down onto the surface of the liquefying ores and fuels and fluxes whilst above, across the bosh, was laterally-wedged the weight of a partially-full furnace stack, known as the burthen or burden, with metallic drops falling through the air-blast onto the near-molten sea below. Delicate pale purple, mauve and pink flames flickered over the surfaces. You may have been lucky enough to see these on a small scale if helping Peter Crew at one of his Bloomery-Smelt weekends in Snowdonia.

The men spoke of the state of smelt getting 'nearer' - meaning that the slag on top was nearer molten - enough to be tapped 'over the notch', that is over the bottom of the slag tap-hole. From very early times, Backbarrow had always had 3 tuyeres at work whereas Newland never had more than 2. From the 1920s the best were made of copper and were hollow with cold water circulating to prevent melt-down. If, when being replaced, their tuyeres jammed, the men used a special hooked gadget which they called a 'baby-snatcher'.

The hearth in 1711 was 2ft x 2ft square 2ft deep, i.e. 8 cubic feet capacity equivalent to 2 tons maximum per cast. By 1770, the hearth had been increased to 2ft x 2ft x 6ft deep, or 24 cubic feet giving a 6 ton cast. The 1888 hearth was 3ft x 3ft x 6ft, but by then a circular cylinder so capacity was 42½ cubic feet, giving a 10 ton cast, which gave 30 tons per day or around 200 tons per week (4 cubic feet of cast iron weigh around 1 ton). The 1911 hearth was 3ft x 3ft x 8ft or 56½ cubic feet, around 300 tons a week.

In 1927 when the furnace went onto coke fuel, the hearth was enlarged to 6ft diameter by 8ft deep, 225cu.ft or 56 tons per cast = 780 tons per week. Its last increase in size was in 1963 when a 17-year 'life' hearth was built, capable of lasting 17 years before needing re-lining. The capacity of its 10ft diameter x9½ft. deep hearth was 2240 tons per week. I climbed into the 1963 double-steel-walled hearth through its tuyere hole and took a shot of the bell at the top of the stack and 2 more of the trapezoid-shaped graphite lining blocks being laid down.

Correspondence files (very extensive over the years), show that a 55ft. tall skip-hoist furnace was to be built about that time, with at least double the capacity of the 1963 hearth. Of course, as we all now know, international changes in the iron and steel industry caused a total flop in UK prices, so the furnace was finally blown out on 23rd Feb. 1966, only 28 months into the 1963 campaign. The site closed in 1967.

An ex-pupil and now colleague of mine, Dr. Sam Murphy, has looked in detail at the turbines on site for English Heritage, and discovered that the smaller unit in size appears to be unique! Putting a key-hole camera inside, the Series 'Y' designation was not a capital letter, but the triple-bladed curved propeller on its drive-shaft. It gave 120hp on a 14ft fall with an open penstock. Built in 1927, it provided power for the blast compressor, hot gases through the stoves and on-site lighting, also water mains pumps for the new larger coke-fired furnace, the two cupolas, the waterlift and the overhead cranes lifting iron in their ladles to pig beds or ingot moulds, and slag to the concrete block-works.

If nothing else, this example serves to tell us that the Charcoal Iron Company was always to the fore with innovation and experiment, with knowledge aforethought and detailed records for those who can 'read' them.

The Correspondence Files deserve a chapter on their own. Much is repetitive detail, such as checking that the three to ten analyses to be done per day were correct, that railway wagons had been unloaded promptly, that orders had been stripe-painted to avoid errors, that the Analyst must be at HQ

Fig. 3. View of works in 1923.

in Lindal (only a 10-mile horse-ride away before their first 'lurry' in 1908 or car in 1911), for at least 3 mornings a week and to check that the scrap dealers on site be removed before the furnace went into blast. There were injured workmen to visit in cottage hospitals, or at the Clovelly Nursing Home in Devon. Both the furnace Foreman, the Analyst and the almost permanent on-site Engineer were each kept extremely busy at three places at once. Some letters were of technical information, or of re-ordering of commodities such as acid batteries. However, some give valuable insights; or were poignant or amusing or even censorious.

The Accidents Ledger was quite a different story from that of the technical side. Even by 1943, there was still only one small tin of bandages on site and one small oil bottle to counteract hot metal in their eyes. There was never any attempt to train the work force. No lectures about 'hot-black' dangers, no hard hats, leather aprons, gloves, or strong steel toe-capped boots although most injuries were caused by dropping a hot pig on their toes. And only the bare minimum of maintenance for severely-injured husbands .

In spite of all that, they were a tight band of local lads and dads who worked long hours with few trade demarcations. It sorrowed me to discover not a single reference to their trades on any gravestone in Haverthwaite churchyard - only one wood turner and one beck-watcher. Perhaps most still had strong self-negatory Quaker links. Workforce family names that featured frequently from 1919-1965 are:-
Backhouse Baines Barker Bell Benson Bevins Bigland Booth Clarke Comthwaite Coulthwaite Coward Dickinson Dixon Edge Edmondson Goodman Jewel Lancaster Oldcom Ormandy Postlethwaite Rogerson Stretch Summers Tyson Ullock and Williamson.

Local firms did most of the tricky plumbing, electrics, building, basketry and general joinery. Tools bought in were made locally. Difficult metalwork was done by the Caird's

Foundry of Barrow, later owned by the Whiles. Local coastal shipping companies were employed to and from Liverpool. Oddly, there was never any mention of the two world wars directly. Of shipping taking pig-iron to North America in WWI, there was never a single mention of convoys or submarines or losses.

In WWII there were some usefully-dated entries in 1941-42 of 'Air Raid Alert' that required the 'damping down of the furnace', yet there was never a hooded cowl at the top of the stack until 1955! It was a go-ahead firm but very idiosyncratic!

Backbarrow suffered two fiascoes, one at each end of World War I, so that the furnace contributed nothing to the nation's war-effort! In 1914, the furnace had gone out of blast in June, expecting to blow-in in mid-November. Unbeknownst to them, a new Ministry of Supplies had moved rapidly, and the fairly new chemical industries of Britain, that roasted tree trunks as the basis for oils, varnishes and paints were promptly switched to making Methanol, a basis for explosives. Forestry pundits in London must have advised the acquiring of all mature coppice and other trees, so that 2000 ton trainloads were sent south to the five largest UK Methanol Plants in Hampshire & Wiltshire. Nobody into local woodland charcoaling had informed Backbarrow of this, and by November all their usual charcoal supplies had disappeared!

The owner, Mr. Jenks, was in despair. One cupola struggled on until June 1915. In 1916, the whole site was put up for sale. It was bought in 1917 by a large family of former charcoal makers from the Midlands, the Whiles, mainly because the women-folk deemed the site "pretty". The men had hoped to set up their own methanol plant, but the government would not help financially, the cost being about £47,000, equivalent to several millions today. So they recouped some of their purchase money by starting a concrete-block works, using the huge slag bank on site and best Portland cement.

At the war's end in late 1918, they discovered that the large methanol factories had stored their waste from the process, which consisted of, of all things, stick and lump charcoal, in barns, paying exorbitant insurance against fire risks! Added to which Sheffield and other major foundry centres had pointed out to the Ministry of Supplies that Backbarrow's iron would have been the very best for making shell cases! The Minister, duly chastened, promptly offered cheap reverse trainloads of 2000 tons of charcoal, to come back to Haverthwaite Station.

By March 1919, the furnace had been relined, cupolas rebuilt, full charcoal sacks were piled everywhere and ore-trains had been ordered. The furnace went into blast in mid-March - and out again promptly in May due to Fiasco No. 2. The 'Jobsworth' Director of Mines would not sign for trainloads of ore, already paid for, to move from Cleator, Florence, and Hodbarrow mines to Backbarrow!

But the While family were of sterner stuff than Mr. Jenks. One swift irate 'phone call to the Minister of Supplies in London, and the trains were on their way within two days.

The new era re-started in June 1919, and was never halted again until 23rd February 1966, when even the British Iron & Steel Corporation was struggling against Far

Eastern prices based on cheap labour. Backbarrow collapsed on that day, only 26 months after putting in their brand-new 17-year hearth. And, as stated, they were working on plans for a second stack some 55ft high with a skip-hoist to make an additional 50,000 tons of high quality iron a year.

As we all know, it never happened.

Acknowledgements

Jack Y. Lancaster of Workington, consultant advisor on blast furnaces to Australia and India; Helen Kaune, Materials Information Co-ordinator, IoMat. For material on Prof. Henry Louis; Jake Almond of the HMS; Ron Lyon, recently retired cupola man from Yorkshire and his ex-colleague, Geoff Lucas, who helped on 'Chills'.

References

Howard E.D: Modern Foundry Practice, London 1942.
Barrow-in-Furness Record Office, . Of the many boxes of MSS seventeen were most valuable and are listed below (all prefixed BDB/2):
/1 - Financial Records 1863-1874,
/2/11-14. Profit & Capital Returns 1946-50,
/5/1 - Iron Ore Ledger 1868-1874,
/9/1-2 - Pig Iron Books 1879-1906,
/12/1 - Analysis of Samples 1897-1920,
/3/2-8 - Company Letterbooks 1908-1920,
/5/18-23 - Materials ordered 1918-1923,
/12/7 - Analysis Furnace Books 1919-1929,
/14/10 - Employees +Wage Rates 1920-1965,
/6/5-27 - List of Ingredients 1925-1955,
/6/28-29 - Technical Details 1929-1939,
/12/10 - Ingot Mould Analysis 1922-1965,

/12/9 - "Leven" iron Analysis 1937-1953,
/14/16 - Wages Books 1953-1965,
/16/1-12 - Correspondence Files 1907-1960s,
/17 - Plans, Sections, Site Photos 1911-1956.
The Duke of Buccleugh MSS is useful for Ingot Mould data at Backbarrow - ref: BDB/47/T63,T70,Bag A56 - 1956-1963.